Liberty or Death

LIBERTY OR DEATH

The story of Thomas Hardy, shoemaker, and
John Cartwright, landowner, in the early
struggles for parliamentary democracy

Ray Hemmings

Lawrence and Wishart
London 2000

Lawrence and Wishart Limited
99a Wallis Road
London
E9 5LN

www.l-w-bks.co.uk

First Published 2000

British Library Cataloguing in Publication data.
A catalogue record for this book is available from the British Library.

ISBN 0 85315 907 6

Typeset in Liverpool by Derek Doyle & Associates.
Printed and Bound in Great Britain by Redwood Books, Trowbridge.

CONTENTS

LIST OF ILLUSTRATIONS

ACKNOWLEDGEMENTS

The numerous quotations from the records of the London Corresponding Society have been taken from Mary Thale's published compilation of the papers of that Society. She has edited these papers with great care and I am most grateful for her generous permission to use the fruits of her labours; also for her permission to quote from her edited version of the *Autobiography of Francis Place*.

I have tried to present events as they may have appeared at the time by quoting from newspaper reports, contemporary autobiographies, etc; but the work also rests on the researches of numerous writers whose books are listed in the bibliography. If they are not acknowledged at every point, this is simply out of a desire to avoid overburdening the text with footnotes.

I am grateful too for the help and encouragement I have received from Professor Brian Simon, and also from Professor John Saville, who offered many helpful suggestions. But of course it was for me to interpret their ideas and therefore the responsibility for any errors remains my own.

R.E.H.

PART I BEGINNINGS

1

In 1761, early in the fifth summer of the Seven Years War, a young naval lieutenant fell into the English Channel from the decks of the King's ship *Magnanine*. Orders were given to launch a lifeboat. It took some little time, however, for the crew members to free the boat of its sheets, to find a replacement for a missing oar, to understand the officers' directions for lowering the boat in such a way that the two oarsmen were not themselves tipped into the main. While all this was being accomplished, the watchers in the stern of the ship realised that the fallen lieutenant could not swim. As he disappeared under the waves for a second time, one of the onlookers, Mr Midshipman John Cartwright, kicked off his boots, stripped himself of his jacket and plunged into the water to seize his brother-officer by the collar just before the poor man disappeared for the third, and probably last, time.

This was the first of Cartwright's rescues, though it was certainly not the last. In fact it became almost a hobby. He hauled two men out of the River Trent as it flowed through his home village of Marnham; and again when he was taking a Sunday afternoon walk with his wife and niece at Enfield, the party spied a boy struggling in the river. Cartwright, now a Major in his fifties, plunged into the flood to rescue his fourth fellow-human from drowning.

But Cartwright was not on hand when seafarer Walter Hardy fell into the Irish Sea in 1760; Walter drowned, leaving his wife alone to rear their eight-year-old son, Thomas – not the Thomas Hardy who hanged Tess of the D'Urbervilles, but one who was destined to become a celebrity by being not-hanged. Thomas's parents had had plans for the boy – he was to have had a good education, to have become a minister of religion, or even a doctor perhaps. But now his widowed mother faced a difficult future and was forced to trim her ambitions for young Thomas. Her father paid out one penny a week for the boy's schooling until he was ten and then took him to learn his own trade as shoemaker which promised a secure, if not exalted, occupation – 'for folk have to be shod'. So Thomas, having learned to read and write, added to his repertoire a more practical range of skills. He learned to cut, to seat, to bottom, to close, to french, to bind – the basics of cobbling which were all his grandfather had ever needed to supply the villagers with strong, plain boots. Later, there not being enough feet in the village to provide two shoemakers with a livelihood, Thomas moved to Glasgow where he was able to acquire those refinements to his trade demanded by the more fashion-conscious townsfolk.

Born into a family of country gentlemen, John Cartwright enjoyed, or endured, a somewhat easier childhood than this. His was a family whose status dated back to Tudor times when an ancestor, Edward Cartwright, had acquired no less than three of the abbeys dissolved by Henry VIII. At a later date family fortunes declined somewhat as a result of backing the wrong side in the Civil War, and they did not greatly revive in the intervening hundred years. John's father found the education of his ten children a difficult burden, though eased by the five girls needing no expensive schooling.

John was the third son. At the age of five he started at Newark Grammar School; but, not demonstrating great academic flair, he soon found himself transferred to the cheap Heath Academy in Yorkshire – a kind of Dotheboys Hall. From here he emerged at sixteen, with, as he said, only a smattering of Latin and no other language but his own. But with a remarkable 'gentleness of disposition', according to his niece (who later chronicled his life).

Maybe, but this gentleness hid a bruised self-image. This is evident in a letter he wrote some years later to his younger brother Edmund who became a classical scholar, a Fellow of Magdalene College, Oxford, a poet and the illustrious inventor of the first steam-powered loom (which, incidentally, deprived a large number of workers of their livelihood). John wrote asking to see some of Edmund's poems: 'Though my soil was early under the care of slothful husbandmen, and has been denied the sunshine of a college: though it has been exposed to ruthless elements, those inveterate foes of human erudition; yet do not altogether consider the produce of a richer soil and happier culture as pearls cast before swine.'

2

Mr Cartwright Snr had decided that John, having finished his schooling, should remain at the family home at Marnham to be trained in agricultural methods and estate management. But, for all his 'gentle disposition', John harboured more adventurous ambitions: one night he packed his knapsack and set off to join the Prussian army of Frederick the Great, then at war with Austria.

He reached no further than Stamford however. Here he was overtaken by the family steward who, impressing upon him the great distress that he was causing his dear parents, persuaded him to retrace his steps. As a quid pro quo, they then facilitated (with the help of his aunt Lady Tyrconnel) his entry into the navy of King George III.

The eighteenth century was not a peaceful one: more often than not Britain was warring with one or more of its European neighbours – Austria, Spain, the Netherlands, France. So it was that Midshipman John Cartwright was plunged straight into battle. Within a month of his enrolment in the Navy he was writing from his first ship, the *Essex*, to his father: 'Honoured Sir ... On Friday we took a French frigate of twenty-two guns ...' He was present at the taking of Cherbourg, after which he was transferred to the *Magnanime*, under the command of Lord Howe – or Black Dick as he was nicknamed by his men.

Lord Howe was a taciturn man whose crew, if they caught a rare smile on his face, would nod to each other – 'Oh-aye, we'll be having some fun in the fighting-way'. Howe was a hero dedicated to battle and for many years John remained one of his most devoted worshippers. It is not so easy to understand what it was in this young midshipman which evoked in Howe a long-lasting paternal fondness. Perhaps his Black Dick persona wearied him and he came to welcome the vicarious relief of Cartwright's boyish enthusiasm for action – whether this took the form of rescuing a fellow officer from the main, or helping to drown Frenchmen. And Cartwright saw plenty of action, especially in the momentous battle of Quiberon Bay in 1759, of which he sent a full account to his aunt, Lady Tyrconnel:

> ... it is impossible for fancy to point out a scene so noble as that of two fleets of men-of-war beginning to engage...We entertained ourselves with viewing the many broadsides which were exchanged, till we were near enough to engage

ourselves...His Lordship spied a ship to leeward, and, pointing to her, told the people she should be theirs...We came close under her quarter...poured in our broadside, after receiving hers...The boarders were called out...We had killed the Admiral and almost every officer with a vast number of his men...We had fifteen killed and about seventy wounded; amongst the former was our second lieutenant, Mr Price...[who] was standing by one of my guns when the shot hit him: it was a 48-pounder and wounded thirteen men out of twenty-six that I commanded ... Your Ladyship's Obedient Servant and dutiful Nephew

John Cartwright

P.S. I wish it were in my power to convey an idea of Lord Howe, but I cannot express it: he is all in all.

The battle turned out to be the Trafalgar of the Seven Years War, decimating the French fleet. The war dragged on, but the supply lines to the French armies in North America were now so weakened that at the end the British were left in control of all the colonised territories from Florida to the St Lawrence.

Cartwright continued under the command of his heroic all-in-all, convoying outwardbound Indiamen, chasing off Frenchmen – sons of the *soupe maigre*, as he called them – until 1762 when he was promoted to lieutenant and put in command of the cutter *Spy*. Four years later he was appointed first lieutenant on the *Guernsey* which was on duty on the Newfoundland station, and he soon found himself deputy to the Governor of the colony. Here he led expeditions making maps of the unexplored interior. But most significant to him personally were his observations of the rapacious developers who were cruelly exploiting the poor Irish labourers and fishermen. They, in their turn, visited brutal treatment upon the aboriginals.

'The Red Indians', Cartwright wrote, 'have no intercourse with Europeans, except a hostile one, which, there is great reason to think, is founded, on their part, upon a just, and, to an uncivilised people, a noble resentment of wrongs. On the part of the English fishers, it is an inhumanity that sinks far below the level of savages. The wantonness of their cruelties towards these poor wretches has frequently been almost incredible.' This spluttering outrage peppered with commas is here addressed to the Governor in some lengthy *Remarks on the Situation of the Aborigines*. Cartwright goes on to illustrate his theme with accounts of two atrocities which would certainly hold their own among the most notorious of our twentieth-century barbarities.

After four years in this uncongenial setting, Cartwright eagerly accepted an invitation to join his old hero, Lord Howe, on board the *Queen* which was about to join battle with the Spanish ships in a war over the disputed Falkland Islands. It is doubtful whether his health was fit for such a campaign, but, fortunately, on this occasion diplomacy successfully eliminated the need for the task force.

So in 1770 Cartwright returned home.

3

While Cartwright was mapping the rivers and lakes of Newfoundland, Thomas Hardy was refining his cobbling skills to meet the more sophisticated tastes in footwear of the Glaswegians.

It was but twenty-odd years since the English redcoats had butchered the Scots fleeing up the glens from Culloden. The Bonnie Prince had returned to France leaving the Hanoverian Georges to sit stubbornly on the English throne. The third of them was now in full blunder, unable to find a set of ministers who could last more than about six months, and troubled by growing discontents.

There was, for instance, Wilkes who was arrested for an attack on His Majesty in the notorious *Number 45* issue of his paper *The North Briton*, and who later succeeded in mobilising enough of the chafing discontent among the nouveau riche to get himself elected to Parliament. Within days the Commons expelled him ('almost my Crown depends on it,' George is said to have cried). There followed riots to the tune of 'Wilkes and Liberty', and the voters of Middlesex promptly re-elected him. He was again expelled and again re-elected.

More serious was the King's deafness to the grievances of the American colonists, which was causing irritation, exasperation and eventually downright hostility amongst the Whig opposition. The notorious Stamp Act, a primitive form of VAT on goods imported into the colonies, provoked more problems than the seven-years-war-weary troops charged with controlling the colonists than could cope with. A motion in the Commons for its full enforcement was ignominiously defeated by 274 votes to 134. The Act was then repealed, and George lost another of his Prime Ministers – Lord Grenville.

The king recalled the ailing William Pitt, who, though honoured for his successful management of the armed forces during the Seven Years War, had lost the royal favour. But now, in 1766, the king was at least pleased with his arguments against party government, and the cabinet he formed was not drawn solely from his own party, the Whigs. It was a 'tessellated pavement, without cement', according to Edmund Burke. Pitt himself was not fit enough for the ardours of ministerial office or for regular attendance at the House of Commons, and so took the sinecure of Lord Privy Seal. To qualify for this he had to be raised to the peerage and became known thenceforward as the Earl of Chatham. It was not a popular move for this 'great commoner'. 'He has had a fall upstairs', wrote Lord Chesterfield, 'and will never be able to stand upon his legs again'.

This turned out to be almost literally true: his gout became so severe that he retired to bed for most of his time in office, and after a mere fifteen months the king had to accept his resignation. He was succeeded by the Duke of Grafton and then, in 1770, more permanently by Lord North.

Chatham's health recovered sufficiently for him to make some notable speeches in the House of Lords in the succeeding years, including contributions to debates about the reform of parliament and later about the American war. It was on one such occasion in 1778 that he collapsed in mid-speech, and within a month he died.

4

One day in 1771 a Mr Ingram, needing some repairs to his shoes, came into the shop where Thomas Hardy worked. In those days a cobbler's shop was often a social meeting-place where gentlemen might spend an hour or two exchanging gossip while their footwear was mended. So it was that, while Thomas was working on Mr Ingram's shoes, he was entertained by their owner's traveller's tales. It turned out that this man was an American colonist who had recently survived fearsome storms during a seven-week voyage from the other side of the world. He described the cities that were growing up in the new continent, he told of the rich fruits they harvested from the land, of the unexplored territories to the west, of the wild Indians and the accursed redcoats who robbed the citizens and raped their women.

When he returned the following week Mr Ingram was so pleased with Thomas's work and so impressed by his obvious intelligence that he was persuaded to offer the young man a tempting position in the new colony. It transpired that Ingram owned a shoe factory in New York and had crossed the ocean to find a man to instal as manager of his proposed new works in Virginia. Hardy questioned the American closely about the details of his business, the conditions of work, the wages that were proposed, the cost of lodgings and so on. His questions showed such acuity that Ingram was convinced he had found the man he sought. The upshot was that he returned a few days later with a draft contract and it was agreed that they would sail together in a month's time in one of those tall-masted ships that Thomas had often watched as they were towed ponderously down the Clyde.

Hardy wrote to tell his mother and grandfather of the news and promised to come to make his farewells in a fortnight. But in less than a week the old man was in Glasgow, the first time in his life that he had moved more than ten miles outside his native village. He had brought the Minister with him, and together they argued that it was Thomas's duty to his mother to stay in the land of his birth. She had lost her husband: it would break her heart to lose her only son too. As to the contract Thomas had signed, that was not valid because he was a minor.

The Minister reinforced this point of law with the word of God. 'The Lord hath said that ye shall honour thy father and thy mother. He hath seen fit to take thy father from us, so thy duty is to thy mother. Ye'll not do this by skittling off across the ocean. Do not be tempted by this man's tales of riches and adventure. The wages of sin is death. Ignore the Word of God and ye shall condemn thyself to the fires of Hell...' The combined force of his grandfather and God overwhelmed young Thomas's resolve. Mr Ingram was told that the contract was invalid, cancelled.

Thomas had already given notice to leave his present employment, and though his employer might well have waived this, he resolved angrily to have no more to do with his grandfather's trade. He left Glasgow and went across country to Carron where he had heard there was work to be had as a bricklayer. And so he began to learn a second trade.

This was Thomas's first gesture of defiance against authority. It must have been hard to accept the loss of fortune and adventure, to stay bound by the dictates of his grandfather. Four years later, however, he came to believe that perhaps after all it had been God's will that he should not cross the ocean. For he learned that Ingram's new factory had become a victim of the English war-makers. As he wrote in his *Memoir*: 'The town was burnt to ashes in one of the mad fits of the British Government at the beginning of the American War'.

This mad fit was probably that described by George Washington in a letter to the Deputy Governor of Rhode Island, which was printed in the English press. He told how the Virginian port of Falmouth was besieged by British ships, and given two hours to move families out of danger. A deputation to the captain of the leading ship learned that he had orders to set fire to all the sea-port towns between Boston and Halifax.

> He would save the town in case we should send off four Carriage Guns, deliver up all our small arms ammunition ... and send four gentlemen as Hostages, which the Town would not do. About half-past nine in the Morning he began to fire from four armed vessels and in five minutes set fire to several houses. He continued firing until after Dark which destroyed the larger part of the Town.[1]

The turning of machines of destruction onto civilian targets is evidently not a twentieth-century invention. In a despatch to the Earl of Dartmouth, Major-General Howe (brother of John Cartwright's admiral hero) described this same firing of Falmouth from the aggressors' point-of-view:

> ... it was found inexpedient to make any attack upon Cape Ann, whereupon they proceeded to Falmouth, which place, after giving timely warning to the inhabitants for the removal of themselves and their effects, was destroyed on 18th October, burning about five hundred houses, fourteen sea-vessels, taking and destroying several others, without any loss on our part.[2]

5

There was more money to be earned from bricks than from boots, but Hardy did not find his new work very congenial. He particularly disliked climbing the ladders that mounted the stages of scaffolding, a rickety structure of wooden poles slung with planks from which the bricklayers worked as the walls grew to the first, second and sometimes to the third storey. When the easterlies swept up the Firth of Forth, Hardy felt as precarious on these swaying and sagging planks as he might have done on the deck of a sailing-ship in a mid-Atlantic gale.

As an apprentice it was his job to keep his mate fed with bricks and mortar which he had to carry up the ladders in a hod on the end of a pole slung over his shoulder. His mate would let him put one or two bricks in place so that he was gradually learning the skill of laying, judging the amount of mortar, getting the brick even with its neighbour. But for most of the long hours of labour, he was simply trudging up and down the ladders clinging on with his one free hand and all the while fearful of missing his step. And then one day what he most feared actually happened. They were working on a house that was destined to become the residence of their boss, Mr Roebuck. They were building the wall up from the first floor. Hardy stepped onto the topmost plank when one of the joints beneath him, a badly tied rope perhaps, gave way. He and his mate were hurled into the basement of the half-built house. His mate was killed outright; but, miraculously, Hardy was dragged out with no more than painful bruising.

Was this another message from God? At any rate, it was enough to persuade Thomas to return to his last. He found work with a cordwainer, James Wilson, who had recently come back from London and was given to entertaining his customers with stories of that great city. As he bent over his work, Thomas listened to these tales as avidly as he had those of Mr Ingram three years earlier. But now he had reached his majority and was not to be denied.

Just a year earlier, Dr Johnson had declared that 'the noblest prospect which a Scotchman ever sees is the high road that leads him to England'. This remark had not, of course, reached Hardy's ear, but he did relish the noble prospect. The high road for him was a fishing-smack, the *Stirling*, which tossed him down the east coast of England and left him eleven days later on the banks of the Thames.

He landed on 23 April 1774, with just eighteen pence in his pocket and a richness of hope in his heart. He set off across London Bridge. Downstream he saw the Tower of London, a sight which increased his excited wonder (though had he been able to see into the future, it would have filled him with foreboding). He made his way towards the dome of St Paul's through streets even more crowded, noisy, dirty and smelly than those of Glasgow. But he was a big man, nearly six foot tall, broad-shouldered and muscular, and he pushed through the crowds with no great difficulty. His greater problem was to find his way to Bush Lane, and the house of Mr Kerr to whom James Wilson had given him a letter of introduction.

6

Four days after Hardy had set foot in London, the Leader of the Whigs, Charles Fox, declared in Parliament the principle that 'countries should always be governed by the will of the governed'. This was a novel idea to most of those who heard him: they were men in the process of building that empire on which the sun would be commanded never to set, and this could not be done on the basis of the fanciful notions that Fox was peddling. Fox's principle did not apply even to Britain itself, where less than one-tenth of the men who were governed, and none of the women, were ever invited to express their will.

The occasion of Fox's extraordinary proposition was a debate on the abolition of the duty on tea imports to America. The will of the colonists on this matter had been made plain the previous year at the Boston tea-party, when they had hurled three-hundred-and-forty chests of tea from the trading ships into the waters of Boston harbour. Their feelings had been expressed more explicitly and with considerable eloquence a year after the tea party, in a petition addressed by a congress of colonists (later to become *the* American Congress) to King George. Their grievances were those of a people suffering the oppressive rule of the military and their petition opened with a list of objections:

—to the use made of the Army whose Commander-in-Chief (General Gage) had been appointed Governor;
—to the officers of Custom being empowered to break into houses with no authority from magistrates;
—to Assemblies being 'repeatedly and injuriously dissolved';
—to the taxes and duties arbitrarily raised;
—to property being often confiscated;
—to the abolition of trial by jury;
—to forfeitures being incurred for slight offences;
—to persons being sent for trial to other colonies, or even to Britain.

All this gives the lie to the story which was put about (preserved in many British history books to this day) that the colonists fought the war of independence simply and solely to avoid paying taxes. They certainly disliked taxes being imposed on them by a parliament in which they had no representation. But this was only one of many injustices to which they felt subjected.

Their petition proceeded to convey in majestic language the outraged feelings of the colonists and to appeal to the King's sense of justice and respect:

> ... in Apprehension of being degraded into a state of Servitude from the pre-eminent rank of English Freemen while our Minds retain the strongest Love of Liberty and clearly foresee the Miseries preparing for us and our Posterity... Feeling as Men and thinking as Subjects in the Manner we do, Silence would be Disloyalty...We ask but for Peace, Liberty and Safety. We wish not a diminution of the Prerogative nor do we solicit the Grant of any new Right in our Favour... Filled with Sentiment of Duty to your Majesty and of Affection to our Parent State, deeply impressed by our Education and strongly confirmed by our Reason... we present this petition only to obtain Redress of Grievances and Relief from Fears and Jealousies.

Evidently General Gage was not governing by the will of the governed; but this principle of Fox's would certainly not have appealed to King George. Indeed, it has been accepted by an Imperial power only quite recently, and then only because that power did not feel itself strong enough to resist. King George did feel strong enough. After talking with General Gage he wrote to his Prime Minister (Lord North): 'He says they will be lions while we are lambs, but if we take the resolute part they will undoubtedly prove very meek.' So he 'took the resolute part' and his only reply to the petition was in the form of bullets.

Not all his subjects saw it this way, however. There was a report in the press, for instance:

> At a Meeting of Seamen at Rotherhithe the brave Tars came to a Resolution not to serve on board any Ship destined for America and they declared that if Press Warrants should be issued out then sooner than be forced like Slaves to fight against the Americans they would die on the Spot.[3]

The American lions failed to exhibit their predicted meekness. It was reported that:

> ... they have appointed a general Fast to be observed throughout the Colonies to implore Success to their Arms ... The people are in the greatest Spirits imaginable owing to a Dutch ship having slipt into one of the unwatched Ports with 1400 Stand of Arms and 400 Barrels of Gunpowder.[4]

In January 1775, the Earl of Chatham proposed a motion of conciliation with the American colonists, but this was defeated in the House of Commons. As was a similar motion proposed by Edmund Burke in the following March. In the now familiar way of weak governments, the King and his Ministers could not abide the notion of conciliation: they were determined to show their leonine strength.

In June came the first major engagement of the war – except that it was not a war as far as Britain was concerned, her soldiers were merely 'putting down a rebellion'. General Gage set out to dislodge the 'rebels' from Bunker Hill and in the process lost nearly half of his own men. The first thousand Englishmen were killed, the first of thirty-four thousand who were to die in the next five years of conflict.

7

John Cartwright was 'unrecognisable' according to his family when he returned from his debilitating exertions in Newfoundland. His once robust frame was now alarmingly emaciated and his doctor prescribed an analeptic pill which 'threw out a smart fit of suppressed gout'. Cartwright ever after considered that he owed his life to this doctor, though according to his niece he 'never afterwards regained his former colour, or the plumpness of figure which he possessed in early youth.'[5]

Cosseted by his family, John entered a period of prolonged convalescence during which he set about patching up his faulty education, reading – and writing. He wrote a lengthy pamphlet – all his writing was lengthy – on the *Rights and Interests of Fishing Companies*. He wrote verbose letters to Miss Anne Dashwood, the young woman whom he intended to marry. He wrote a *Plan for the perpetual Supply of English Oak for the Royal Navy* which he submitted to the Government and then spent ten years unsuccessfully trying to get adopted by them. And in 1774 he wrote his first political tract, *American Independence: the Glory and Interest of Great Britain*. This he amended and republished the following year in the form of *A Letter to Edmund Burke Esq.*, though he explained to Miss Dashwood that because 'it may possibly be displeasing to the Government, I do not wish at present to be known as the Author – I am not afraid of the Law but I should be glad of advancement in my profession'.

If by his profession he meant the navy, his tract would certainly not have helped. His main proposition was that there should be a union between the home country and America, with separate legislatures, which would have given an independence to the colonies, including the right to raise their own taxes. This would certainly have been enough to 'displease the Government'. But there were still more subversive ideas in his pamphlet. His arguments about conditions in the colonies led him to reflect on the political arrangement at home. The corrupt state of government and parliament, he asserted, denied people their fundamental freedom. And this freedom was no gift contingent on grants and charters, custom and usage: it was not the Magna Carta, nor the settlement of 1688 that gave Englishmen their liberty. Freedom was 'the immediate gift of God ... It is not derived from any one, but is original in every one; it is inherent and inalienable ... It is impossible that any human being can be without a title to liberty, except he himself has forfeited it by crimes'.

It was on the basis of this uncompromising assertion that, during the next forty years of his life, Cartwright argued the case for constitutional reform. He had acquired a mission. Why did this man, sprung from the conventional culture of landed gentry, suddenly seize the cap of liberty and wear it with such serious and obstinate perseverance for the rest of his life? 'Mine was a Tory family I am told, and Popery was once its religion; but as for myself, I shall be neither Papist nor Tory, until I can believe in the infallibility of popes and kings'.

The second edition of this subversive tract was at the printers when Cartwright accepted an appointment as Major of the Nottinghamshire militia, not the most obvious position for a man with libertarian pretensions. The militia was a kind of territorial army. It was intended to act as an armed police force to maintain law and order, being at the disposal of local magistrates when, not infrequently, they were faced with outbursts of 'civil unrest'. Each regiment of the militia was under the nominal command of the local Lord Lieutenant: the chain of command passed through lieutenant-colonel to colonel to major. But in Nottinghamshire real responsibility rested with the major, his seniors rarely showing any interest in local proceedings.

Cartwright was proud of this new position – he retained the title 'Major' for the rest of his life, long after he had ceased service with the militia. He was proud too of his regiment which he was determined to build up to be a serious and efficient unit. He established a tradition of 'undeviatingly strict' (though humane) discipline. The strictness was usual in the professional Army and Navy, but humaneness was not generally seen as either necessary or desirable. In other regiments of the militia both qualities seem to have been rare.

One of Cartwright's first acts was to design a new regimental button, which became a feature of the uniform. The design is interesting: 'it consists of a cap of liberty resting on a book, over which appears a hand holding a drawn sword in its defence. The motto is "Pro legibus et libertate", "For our laws and liberty".'

The militia was certainly there to uphold the law, but the defence of liberty was not usually seen as one of its prime tasks. More commonly it was engaged in the defence of property, of the little fortunes that local squires had made or inherited and were hoping to enlarge. Perhaps it was to this liberty, the freedom to enrich oneself, that the Nottinghamshire Colonel assumed the new regimental button to refer.

But if Cartwright felt no contradiction between his political and military activities, things became more complicated when he heard that his old hero, Admiral Lord Howe, who had been given command of His Majesty's naval forces across the Atlantic, was about to invite his young admirer to serve as a lieutenant in this navy. It put Cartwright in a turmoil of conflicting loyalties. How could he bring himself to refuse the opportunity to serve under his old hero? What would Lord Howe think of him if he did? Yet how could he command men to fire their cannons at the American colonists while at the same time publishing pamphlets upholding the justice of the colonists cause?

After some agonised days and nights he went to see the great man 'with a very full and disturbed mind' – so much so that he found himself unable to explain himself properly. The best he could do was to leave Lord Howe with a letter that he had already prepared. But it was written in such convoluted language that the Admiral may not have had the patience to fathom its submerged meaning. Cartwright anxiously awaited a reply. Three days later he sent his Lordship a copy of his pamphlet with a covering note revealing himself as the author. Eventually the answer came:

> Lord Howe presents his compliments to Mr Cartwright. He is favoured with the pamphlet referred to in his note. He thinks opinions in politics ... are to be treated like opinions in religion, whereon he would leave everyone at liberty to regulate his conduct by those ideas which he had adopted upon due reflection and inquiry ...

Thus Howe accepted Cartwright's reasons for not wanting to join the fleet that was to blockade and try to bombard the Americans into submission. A tolerant letter, but it still left Cartwright with gnawing misgivings that perhaps he had not presented himself in a wholly honourable light. He wrote again, this time adopting the same third-person convention that Lord Howe had used. He confessed to 'a considerable uneasiness ... an apprehension that Lord Howe had misinterpreted his motive for sending the pamphlet'. And so he 'took the liberty of once more intruding on his Lordship's time' with a few more pages of obsequious explanations. In a short reply Lord Howe explained that his previous letter had been one of twenty-four he had written that day, so he could not remember what he had written that might have caused such uneasiness. He assured the young man that his was a 'friendship he wishes to retain'.

There is an ironic sequel to this little story. At a later date, after the authorship of the *Letter to Edmund Burke Esq* had become public, Cartwright was offered a command in the American navy! This he declined, explaining that 'though I would never consent to bear arms against the liberties of America, I considered that nothing could absolve a man from the duty he owed his own country, and that I would stick by the old ship as long as there was a plank of her above water'.

So Cartwright turned his attention back to his regiment of militia, and with such diligence that in July 1776 he was presented with the freedom of the City of Nottingham. He also found time to produce a little book, *Take your choice*, in which he laid out the ideas for parliamentary reform which were to form the basis for his life's crusade. The 'choices' that he offered were summed up in a legend on the title page:

TAKE YOUR CHOICE	
Representation and Respect	Imposition and Contempt
Annual parliaments and Liberty	Long Parliaments and Slavery

The alternatives in the top half of the table refer both to the property qualifications by which a man was judged fit to vote and to the lop-sided structure of the parliamentary constituencies in which, for instance, the growing conurbations in the Midlands returned no members whilst many groups of forty men or fewer in Cornwall had two representatives (see chapter 16 below). Indeed less than 10 per cent of the adult male population, and of course no women, qualified to vote at that time in Britain.

Cartwright argued for equal constituencies in the larger towns, with representation in proportion to the number of voters, and for a separate County list which would include the smaller towns. He also advocated giving the vote to all men over the age of 18, excluding criminals and lunatics. (Women he considered did not need to vote because their husbands would represent their views!)

But although he did not consider property to be a condition for franchise, Cartwright certainly thought it necessary for a Member of Parliament. He would require County candidates to have an estate and an income of at least £400 p.a.; and a town candidate would have to have £9000 worth of property or an income of £300 or more. (A skilled worker could not expect to earn much more than £100 p.a. at this time.) So although Cartwright wanted all and sundry (men) to be given the vote, he certainly could not stomach the idea of admitting the hoi-poloi into the Counsels of State.

The lower half of Cartwright's title-page table, which promises liberty in place of slavery, refers to the seven-year life that a parliament then enjoyed. Cartwright was writing at a time when Britain was staggering under a heavy national debt (a carryover from the Seven Years War) and when war in the American colonies was brewing. Such things would not be allowed to happen, he thought, if Parliament was accountable to its electorate every year.

All of this was founded on a version of history whose origins have been traced, notably by Christopher Hill, to before the seventeenth century (and it was still in currency until well into the nineteenth century).[6] During the civil war the Levellers were using this historical interpretation to represent British rulers – King and nobility – as inglorious inheritors of the Norman invaders who had appropriated land and riches from the indigenous Anglo-Saxons. They had imposed their alien yoke on a people who, so the story went, had previously enjoyed the rights and liberties established in King Alfred's 'golden reign'. This was a version of history well-suited to the Levellers' purposes, to re-establish 'lost freedoms'; and as Hill points out, they were able to advance from this position to a 'momentous transition: from the recovery of rights which used to exist to the pursuit of rights because they ought to exist: from historical mythology to political philosophy.'

Cartwright employed this mythology and philosophy, though of course he was no Leveller: indeed, coming from a family of landed gentry, and later becoming the owner of a large estate in Lincolnshire, he would surely have been regarded by the Levellers as a part of the 'yoke'. But this did not prevent him from adopting the same version of history and a similar political philosophy, at least as regards what he called 'God-given rights'. In fact by his time this historical construction had become an orthodoxy among radical reformers, wielding as it did the persuasive power that myths so often hold.

8

In his *Memoir*, Thomas Hardy commented that he did not come to London to pursue 'what is falsely called a life of pleasure', and apologised to his readers for not being able to entertain them with the adventures that such a life might have provided. No, this young man (he wrote in the third person) was of a 'contemplative and serious turn of mind'. He clung to the religious faith in which he had been reared, joining a group of Dissenters who met in Crown Court, Covent Gardens. It was quite a large company of very respectable men and women 'of the middle and lower classes' who, he notes, could afford to pay their pastor, Mr Cruden, a considerable salary.

In the country as a whole, the Dissenting community, if such a diversity of sects – Baptists, Presbyterians, Methodists, Calvinists, Quakers, Unitarians, Anabaptists – can be so called, tended at this time towards radical activism. For a hundred years or so they had accepted the limited religious toleration which had come to replace the earlier active persecution. From time to time they had tried to promote the repeal of the Test-and-Corporation Acts which excluded men who were not prepared to receive the Sacrament within the Established Church from municipal office and official positions under the Crown. The benefits of higher education were also limited to those who would subscribe to the

Articles of Religion (of the same Church) – or to those who could afford to go to Scottish or continental universities.

These restrictions fed a festering discontent articulated notably by a group calling themselves 'Rational Dissenters' which grew out of coffee-house meetings in the 1760s and 1770s. The name reflected the scientific and philosophical interests of the participants among whom were, for instance, Benjamin Franklin and Joseph Priestley, James Burgh (whose three volumes of *Political Disquisitions* became seminal to the group), Richard Price (who later provoked Burke into his intemperate attack on the Jacobin supporters of the French Revolution) and, curiously, James Boswell.[7]

The Rational Dissenters were one of several radical groups that became active as the conflict with the American colonists loomed out of the murky corners of palace and cabinet into the brighter light of public consternation. Extra-parliamentary debate buzzed in the Society of Honest Whigs, the London Revolution Society, the Bowood Circle, and the Society for Constitutional Information. These groups were peopled by educated gentlemen, many of them Dissenters, men powerful in commerce and industry, landed gentry, persons of rank and consequence – among them were Lord Shelburne, the Duke of Portland, the Marquis of Carmarthen and some Members of Parliament ... But the flurry rippled downwards as well as upwards. It certainly reached the Sunday meetings in Covent Gardens, where sermons acquired a political slant, and chins wagged with protesting fervour as the congregation lingered after the services. And in his cobbler's shop, Thomas Hardy heard the gentlemen, as they waited for their boots, exchange opinions about the latest newspaper reports:

> At a meeting of 500 freeholders of the County of Middlesex at the Mile End Assembly Rooms ... Mr Masters ... declaimed against the Ministry for their Conduct respecting America; their sending the sons of Englishmen there to cut the Throats of Englishmen ... We are called upon to redouble our Attention and Zeal for the Defence and Preservation of all our constitutional Rights from seeing the Iron Hand of Oppression extended to our Fellow-Subjects on the other side of the Atlantic (*Northampton Mercury*, 2 October 1775).

> The King's Address to the Lords ... They openly avow their Revolt, Hostility and Rebellion. They have raised Troops and are collecting a Naval Force. They have seized the Public Revenue ... a Torrent of Violence ... the Authors

and Promoters of this desperate Conspiracy ... I have acted with the same temper anxious to prevent the effusion of the Blood of my Subjects ... To be a Subject of Great Britain is to be the freest Member of any Civil Society in the known World (*Northampton Mercury*, 26 October 1775).

Lord George Cavendish opened the Address ... The Lord Mayor called the War against the Americans a murderous War and he would consider every Subject that fell on either side as assassinated by the Minister ... The Debate continued till after Four on Friday morning ... On Division there were 278 votes cast for the Address and 108 against it (*Northampton Mercury*, 28 October 1775).

9

Thomas Hardy, hearing the gentlemen in his cobbler's shop discussing the latest (though three months old) items of news from the American battlefields, thought literally 'there but for the Grace of God ...' Politics were the general topic of conversation, he recalled in his *Memoir*, adding of his youthful and inexperienced self, 'his heart always glowed with the love of freedom and was feelingly alive to the sufferings of his fellow creatures'.

But he had other preoccupations, too. For one thing he had found himself a wife, Lydia Priest, the daughter of a carpenter from Chesham.[8] They married in 1781 and over the next dozen years she bore him six children. None survived more than a few years and the last, stillborn, 'found a grave with its hapless mother'. The circumstances surrounding this sadness are a part of the climax of this story – which was shortly to lurch Thomas in a direction of which he had no inkling at this time.

Thomas was employed as foreman in the shoemaker shop of one William Barclay, though he appears to have been more involved with the affairs of the little community of Dissenters in Hoxton which he had joined. In 1784 their minister, Mr Cruden, died. He had been a revered figure responsible for much of the growth and steadfastness of the congregation. For a time after his death they were served by a succession of visiting preachers of mediocre calibre. Numbers dwindled. Then, one Sunday, the Scottish accents of a visiting preacher, Mr

Chambers, stirred the flagging hearts of the faithful. Hardy was so uplifted that he wrote to ask Mr Chambers if he might accept a call if one were given. Only if it came from a majority of the Society, was the reply. And so Hardy plunged into his first, perhaps rather fumbling, experience of political manoeuvring.

He was appointed chairman of a sizeable group of those who had been impressed with this preacher and after a couple of meetings he led a deputation to the Elders to request a General Meeting to consider calling Mr Chambers. The Elders, however, were not enthusiastic. They insinuated that there was some unspecified defect in the candidate's moral character. Hardy and his friends were outraged at this vague slur and the Society split into passionately opposed factions. Perhaps the Elders were tipped off by the Almighty; but whatever the source, the intelligence appears to have been so tenuous that for two years they were obliged to maintain a precarious opposition while the pro-Chambers party gathered testimonials from far and wide affirming the purity of their candidate.

Eventually the Elders (after 'ransacking all quarters,' in Hardy's words) saw fit to point their finger without ambiguity. There were, they affirmed, two Mrs Chambers – one in Scotland and one in England. In those days such an irregularity might have escaped legal action, but it could not avoid the censure of such a morally fastidious group as these Dissenters. A bigamous minister, indeed! Case dismissed.

10

Parliamentary reform was not a live issue when *Take your choice!* first appeared and there was not yet any very widespread support for Cartwright's view of the American war. Immediately after the Declaration of Independence (1776), the British forces seemed to be getting the upper hand. The battles for New York in August put Washington's troops into retreat. The following year the British commander Cornwallis entered the city of Philadelphia. However, the redcoats' victorious run did not last. After the bloody defeat of General Burgoyne's army in Canada, the following letter, dated 19 October 1777, was received (by way of France) on 11th December:

To the Honorable President of the Council of the States of Massachusetts Bay

Sir,

I have the Pleasure to send your Honorable Council the enclosed Copy of a Convention by which Lieut-Gen. Burgoyne surrendered himself and his whole Army the 17th instant into my hands. They are now upon their March towards Boston...I am so extremely busy in pursuing the Army forward to stop the cruel Career of General Vaughan up Hudsons River that I have only time to acquaint you that my friend General Lincoln's Leg is on a fair way to doing well ...

Horatio Gates[9]

Mr Wilson, Surgeon to General Burgoyne's army, gave the same news (but for the state of Gen. Lincoln's leg) from the British side, in a letter home dated 15th October:

Tomorrow our capitulation is to be signed but I expect to remain with the Hospital and the Wounded which are almost beyond number. I fear to say we have near 600 and I think the Provincials must have more though I hear they have very few Surgeons. I believe there hardly was ever known such Carnage.

The French, perhaps looking for ways to recoup their losses in the Seven Years War and always ready to seize a chance to make things difficult for the British, had been giving a helping hand to the Americans ever since the Declaration of Independence and had recognised them as an independent country. The Spanish too saw their chance to mop up some of the islands of the West Indies. Now American successes encouraged these old enemies, and at the beginning of 1778 the French signed treaties of Commerce and Alliance with the new country. Effectively this meant that the old wars were resumed (though without the formality of an actual declaration), bringing hostilities uncomfortably close to home. In August 1779 French and Spanish ships were sighted in the Channel and Sir Charles Hardy (no relation to Thomas, of course) sailed out to engage them. Unfortunately, unfriendly winds carried his ships out to the west and a fleet of sixty-three enemy sail arrived off the Lizard unmolested. Press reports of the day describe the confusion that followed:

Aug 12: ... the combined Fleets of France and Spain have blocked up Plymouth Harbour.

Aug 15: Nothing but Military Movements are going forward...Camps here and there and everywhere ... Messages have been sent from the War Office to the Lord Lieutentants of the Counties westward of London to hold themselves in readiness. Orders have been given by his Grace the Duke of Northumberland to all Grooms, Postillions &c in the Kings Stables to learn the Military Exercises along with Volunteer Tradesmen &c of Westminster...The Press Gangs made another haul of about 200 men on Tuesday Night ... Upwards of 80000 men are now in Arms in England alone.

Aug 17: The Alarm ... was very great this Day among the Merchants of the Change ... An Address to the King from the Nobility, Gentry and Freeholders of the County of Devon declared that ... should our Enemies be daring enough to make an Attempt to invade this Kingdom they will be ready to assist in repelling such an Attack.

Aug 24: Since the Departure of the Combined Fleets we are nearly as much subject to Doubt and Fluctuation in our Intelligence as you are in London. The last Reports are that the Fleets were off Fowey. This however is not believed ... Orders have been issued that in the case of a Bombardment the Pavements should be taken up and removed that the Bombs should sink into the Earth without bursting. Two French Men of War came inshore at Dartmouth under English Colours and made a Signal for 2 boats to come off with Provisions, which was complied with. The French paid for the Provisions and sent the boats on shore again.[10]

The alarm eventually subsided when the warships sailed off after one half-hearted and unsuccessful attempt at invasion. The King ordered a public Fast, 'that Almighty God will vouchsafe a special Blessing on our Arms'. But the fear of invasion was not totally quenched until the French fleets had been decimated at Trafalgar twenty-five years later.

At the other end of the country the gentlemen of Yorkshire were less panicked by these flurries. Nor were they so much moved by the victories or the defeats of King George's armies across the ocean, or by the agonies of the untended wounded and dying – no, for them, it was the damned expense of it all. The national debt was rising, prices were rising, and above all taxes were rising. It was this state of affairs that prompted the Reverend Christopher Wyvill to call together the Yorkshire Association – Gentlemen, Clergy and Freeholders. Wyvill's view was that the war, which these taxpayers had to pay for, should never have been allowed to happen – and would not have been allowed to happen but for the corrupt state of Parliament. The gentlemen were agreed on the folly and evil of the war and were only too ready to accept Wyvill's persuasive explanation as to the cause. They determined to send a petition to Parliament demanding an end to this 'expensive and unfortunate War', which had added to the national debt, and caused 'a heavy Accumulation of Taxes, and a rapid Decline of Trade, Manufactures and Land Rents'. They also urged the 'Honourable Commons' to 'correct the gross Abuses in the Expenditure of Public Money', and to abolish sinecures and 'Exorbitant Emoluments ... whence the Crown has acquired great and unconstitutional Influence which if not checked may prove fatal to the Liberty of this Country'.

Thus this petition was in accordance with John Cartwright's view that the war against the American colonists was the lamentable result of a corrupt parliament and a faulty constitution. But the reforms that Wyvill and his gentlemen were proposing seemed feeble to Cartwright. However, the Yorkshire Association's protest found more sympathisers than Cartwright had ever attracted, and soon the gentry of one City or County after another were meeting together to add their voice: Middlesex, Winchester, Huntingdonshire, Sussex, Surrey, Essex, Hereford, Nottingham, Cockermouth, Weymouth, Newcastle, Hampshire, Bedford, Exeter, Bristol, Dorset, Norfolk...

What could the Commons do in response to this avalanche? Not a few of the members were beneficiaries of the abuses that were being complained of, and most of them, secure in their seats for seven years, were unready to consider reducing their tenure to three years as was proposed. What they did was what politicians generally to do under such circumstances. They passed a resolution. It was proposed by one Mr Dunning, pithily worded and with suitable militancy; it deflected the blame almost into the abstract, declaring: 'That the influence of the Crown has increased, is increasing, and ought to be diminished'.

And then they did nothing.

At this point Charles James Fox, the Whig leader, decided that it would be politic (precisely that) to appoint a committee to prepare a programme for reform. But however serious this initiative was made to look, privately Fox was saying: Whenever anyone proposes to you a specific plan of reform, always answer that you are for nothing short of annual parliaments and universal suffrage; then you are safe.

The committee – known as the Westminster Committee – in turn appointed a sub-committee which was to do the work. Fox of course wanted to out-Wyvill Wyvill and made sure that there was a strong radical representation in the group. Richard Brinsley Sheridan, the playwright, who was already active politically, was appointed chairman, and among its members was John Cartwright, author of that radical pamphlet *Take your choice!*

Earlier that year Cartwright had been adopted as a candidate for parliament by the Whig burgesses of Nottingham. He had been invited to put his name forward two years before, but on that occasion another candidate had been chosen. Now he was a prospective candidate and he had already been chosen by the great Charles Fox to work on a parliamentary committee. Naively, he saw himself a framer of policy, on a behind-the-scenes think-tank. This was not exactly the way Fox saw it.

The sub-committee presented a report whose recommendations closely matched the proposals in *Take your choice!*. It called for annual parliaments, equal electoral districts, universal male suffrage (though with some ambiguity as to what was meant by universal), secret ballots, the abolition of property qualifications for members of the Commons and payment for members. This hopelessly radical document was published, but when it came to a parliamentary resolution all that survived was:

> That annual parliaments are the undoubted right of the people of England; and that the act which prolonged their duration was subversive of the constitution, and a violation, on the part of the representatives, of the sacred trust reposed in them by their constituents.

Even this was defeated, as no doubt Fox intended. But there was one important outcome.

Cartwright's conversations with his fellow members of the Westminster Committee encouraged him to go ahead with his idea of a Society dedicated to gathering support for constitutional reform in the country at large. This, at least, was Cartwright's objective, but it was too subversive for some of his proposed founding members. They preferred to define the society's intention as educative; accordingly, it was named the Society for Constitutional Information (SCI).

To its original members the one-guinea annual subscription was not difficult to find: they included three Dukes, three Earls and three Lords, fourteen members of the Commons, several Aldermen. The Rev. Wyvill was there, as were the playwright/politician Richard

Sheridan, Dr Richard Price, Dr Jebb and Thomas Brand Hollis. Who was not to be found among these well-meaning reformers? Notably, not Fox. Nor Pitt, although he was shortly to introduce a mild reforming Bill (which would be thrown out). Nor Wilkes. And certainly not the likes of Thomas Hardy! Hardy was still an unknown; and in any case the subscription would have been too much for him.

So the SCI set out to educate the British people on their proper inheritance of political freedom – largely lost – by publishing for free distribution some older works of political philosophy, together with pamphlets written by SCI members. The first of these, *A Declaration of Rights*, was a statement of the principles that inspired the SCI, or at least those that inspired its author, Cartwright. His writing was becoming rather less dense; at times, in fact, quite pithy: 'To be a MAN is, at all times and in all countries a title to LIBERTY; and he who does not assert it deserves not the name of a MAN.'

Cartwright later heard that the great Lord Chatham, the Elder Pitt, had read this little work with approval. 'Aye this is right; this is very right', he had said to General Oglethorpe. Gleefully, Cartwright relayed this comment to the wavering Wyvill: 'These words', he wrote, 'the General reported to Mr Granville Sharp and myself, at Mr William Sharp's in the Old Jewry'.

11

One of the customers with whom Thomas Hardy struck up an acquaintance was the notorious Lord George Gordon. In fact Hardy claimed more than a mere acquaintance; he was 'very intimate' with him, he said, 'though by no means an approver of his wilder schemes'. On one occasion he invited Lord George to come to hear a Mr Bean preach at the Crown Court Chapel. Mr Bean was a young Scot with whom Hardy had been very impressed.

Lord George accepted the invitation but, unfortunately, not only was Hardy unable to attend chapel on that occasion but neither did Mr Bean appear as expected. His place was taken by a man who *read* his sermon, and read it in a grindingly monotonous manner. This was insupportable to one of Lord George's temperament and he very soon interrupted the dreary discourse to declare that it was contrary to the rules of the Kirk of Scotland for a minister to read his sermon from the pulpit. The congregation may have agreed with the sentiment, but they could not tolerate so unmannerly an intervention from a stranger, and an angry confusion followed. Lord George called for Hardy to come to his aid and, discovering his absence, supposed his friend to have played a trick on him. He left in no sweet temper. The congregation for their part presumed Hardy had sent Lord George there to create a disturbance. The Minister resumed his reading. Meanwhile at home Hardy was innocently helping his wife nurse a sick child.

One of Lord George's 'wilder schemes' led to the deaths of at least 300 Londoners and landed him in the Tower. Ostensibly, the trigger for this violent convulsion was the government's attempt to remove the repressive restrictions placed on Catholics in Scotland. The so-called Relief Act, which removed restrictions in England and Wales, had already passed through Parliament in 1778, with only sour grumbles from the Protestant majority. The notion of a similar bill for Scotland stirred angry passions in that Calvinist province, but seemed an issue unlikely to fuel the outrage of Londoners. But that was to reckon without the ambitions of Lord George who, though not himself greatly moved by religious fervour, eagerly seized on the issue to put himself at the centre of a political crusade. For he was a man consumed with grudges, one who felt himself unheeded. He was a poorly treated younger son of a wealthy family who had gone into the navy but resigned his commission when he was refused the promotion he thought he deserved. Subsequently, having got himself elected to parliament for one of the Wiltshire pocket boroughs, he found to his chagrin that his frequent aggressive interventions in the House had little impact.

Now he would not be spurned. 2nd June 1780 was to be his day. He was then to present a petition to parliament demanding the repeal of the offending Relief Act. This petition, he claimed, contained 120,000 signatures and for added emphasis he asked the Protestant Association to furnish him with at least 20,000 supporters. Possibly twice this number gathered in St George's Fields, over the river from Westminster. They were all given blue cockades and, with Lord George at their head, they set off to march on the Houses of Parliament, their numbers augmented en route by many ungodly ruffians ready and eager for trouble.

It happened, ironically, that the Lords were due that afternoon to debate the Duke of Richmond's motion calling for annually elected Parliaments and for manhood suffrage. Thus the Peers and Bishops found themselves having to force their way through a very unfriendly throng to reach the Upper House. Not all of them arrived unscathed. In fact a number were dragged from their coaches and all but lynched.

Meanwhile Lord George was in the lower chamber presenting his petition. From time to time he came out to the lobby where he reported progress, or lack of it, to the thirty or forty of his supporters who had forced their way that far. 'Lord North calls you a mob!' he told them. None of this mob penetrated the debating chamber itself, although when that seemed threatened some gentlemen drew their swords to defend the narrow entry: one of them promised to run his blade through Lord George's body if any of his 'rascally adherents' came that far. But if the rabble could not get into the Chamber, nor could the members inside get out. This impasse was eventually resolved by the arrival of a contingent of the Cavalry who managed to draw off the crowd enough to allow the Members of Parliament to escape. But all this was only the curtain-raiser to four days of extraordinary violence.

At 11 o'clock that night the Popish chapel of St Anselm and St Cecilia, known as the Sardinian chapel, was destroyed by fire. The Bavarian Chapel suffered the same fate. Other sections of the now drunken mob turned their attention on the houses of known Catholics. The magistrates did not allow the military to interfere with this swelling tide of destruction. The crowds prevented the fire engines, such as they were, to operate except to protect neighbouring (Protestant) houses.

On the second night a frenzied crowd fired the massive gates of Newgate Prison and once inside they dragged terrified prisoners from their cells. The inmates of Fleet Prison were similarly liberated, as were those in the Borough Clink in Deadman's Place. The mobs were now rampaging through the city, looting indiscriminately, emptying any wine cellars they found, demanding money. It was not only Catholics who were now at risk, but any figures of authority, any suspected of siding with the Papists, any who would not join the cries of 'No Popery', any who refused the blue cockade.

Eventually the magistrates, seeing the prospect of their entire city in flames, agreed to let the military take a hand, and on the fourth night, when the crowds converged on the Bank of England, they were met by volleys of musketry. As one of the soldiers wrote afterwards: 'Figure to yourself every man, woman and child in the streets, panic-struck, the atmosphere red as blood, muskets firing in every part ... The business was soon settled near the Bank, but the populace then fell upon lesser game. Private houses in different parts were being ransacked...'[11]

When order was finally restored, gallows were erected in various parts of the city ready for the 59 men who were quickly tried and sentenced. Petitions saved 39 of these but the remainder were strung up near the scenes of their ravages.

Lord George was taken off to the Tower and charged with High Treason. His trial was deferred till the following February and then the impassioned eloquence of the young Thomas Erskine convinced the jury that his Lordship had no malicious intent when he gathered those 40,000 people together on that sweltering day in June. The rioters were not his supporters. None of those sentenced to death had signed his petition. After twenty consecutive hours of evidence and argument, the jury retired at 4 o'clock in the morning and needed only half-an-hour to agree on the prisoner's innocence.

Erskine's skill (later to be applied to more worthy causes) had saved Lord George. But six years later this sad rebel was serving a five-year sentence in the re-built Newgate prison – three of them for publishing a libellous pamphlet and another two for libelling Marie Antoinette! He would have been released had he been able to find the £15,000 security for his good behaviour (for 14 years). But he languished in Newgate until he succumbed to a 'jail-fever' epidemic. He died on 1 November 1793. This was just one year before his one-time friend Thomas Hardy was himself on trial for High Treason, also to be defended by the same Thomas Erskine.

The Gordon Riots, as they were known, remained a scar on the collective unconscious of Londoners; they were a demonstration of the bloody mayhem that could be unleashed with the slightest of provocations. A dozen years later the near-paranoid reactions of Pitt's government to reports of the Terror raging in Paris – and the support that greeted its repressive measures – may well have been influenced by nervous memories of these riots.

12

On 12th November 1780 Major John Cartwright obtained the hand of Anna Katherine Dashwood, eldest daughter of Samuel Dashwood, Esq. of Well Vale, in Lincolnshire. 'To this lady's unceasing care and tenderness, it may be said, that, under Providence, he was indebted for the prolongation of his days beyond the usual period of the age of man ... She administered to his comfort to the last moments of his existence.' So wrote his niece, Frances Cartwright.

Cartwright had courted Anne Dashwood for over nine years; and their marriage was followed by forty-four years of 'domestic Harmony and comfort'. They had no children of their own. However, in 1786 Edmund, the younger brother, whose intellectual power John had so envied, lost his wife, and John adopted his daughter, Frances, giving her the home which Edmund evidently felt unable to provide. This arrangement was not as unusual as it would be today. John himself when he was six years old had been a candidate for adoption by a rich gentleman who, having produced no heirs, asked John's father if he might spare him 'that fine little white-haired fellow.' John was always grateful for his father's refusal but for which he felt he might have been brought up 'as a mere fox-hunting squire of fortune.' Whatever she felt about her own father, Frances came to admire and revere her uncle, rewarding him posthumously with a laudatory, not to say sycophantic, biography.

So 1780 was a significant year for John Cartwright. Apart from his marriage, he launched the Society for Constitutional Information (SCI) in April of that same year. The launching of the Society was probably John Cartwright's most significant public act. In fact, apart from publishing books and pamphlets and rescuing people from drowning, it was perhaps the *only* thing he actually achieved in what is now called the public domain. But as it turned out he gave the infant Society into the care of other (not very competent) hands shortly after its birth.

In a letter to his wife shortly after their marriage, he affected some surprise that the Society should 'do me the honour to call me its founder', writing that 'in that character my name was enrolled in its proceedings when I was absent, and my health drunk as such'. But he added: 'Our society bids fair in time to become a constellation of genius and patriotism'. By patriotism he did not mean, of course, leaping to the colours at every call – he still opposed the American war which continued its uncertain course – but rather the devotion to the struggle to regain the people's rights, as he would have put it. Nevertheless he *was* committed to the Englishman's duty to defend his native land and he continued to nurture his Nottinghamshire militia – 'For our laws and liberty'.

Cartwright spent the summer of 1780 in camp with the militia and after his marriage he took his wife with him to Gosport where the regiment was encamped. They spent most of the year there until the news of his father's death brought them back to Nottingham.

The eldest son George inherited the Marnham estate. But he promptly put it up for auction, since he planned to emigrate to Labrador and had, moreover, just lost a lot of money in an unfortunate speculation. So John borrowed enough to buy the estate himself and for the next few years most of his energies went into rescuing this decaying property, frequently working an eleven-hour day despite his 'shattered constitution', as he himself described it.

He thus had little time to devote to politics and left the SCI to stagger uncertainly through its first few years under the guidance of a rather profligate secretary. A great many pamphlets were published and distributed freely, which certainly helped to get the Society known, but nearly ruined it financially. Membership had grown fairly quickly to 130, but from 1783, as hopes for reform seemed to fade, so the membership declined.

The prospect of asserting control over the American colonists was also receding and by 1783 it was clear that the only option for Britain was to salvage as much as possible from the debris. In April of that year the 'monstrous coalition' was formed: the Tory Lord North and his old Whig adversary Charles Fox joined a cabinet headed by the Duke of Portland, one as Home Secretary and the other Foreign Secretary. Fox had been regarded as an ally of the reformers. Had he not fathered the Westminster committee? Would he not one day see its radical recommendations onto the statute books? Many of the SCI members, who had not rumbled the devious politician in him, were dismayed by his cynical alliance with the diehards. Some clung desperately to their hopes but that cruellest month dealt them a further blow when the Younger Pitt's modest proposals for parliamentary reform were defeated in the Commons.

Hope revived somewhat in November when, after signing a peace treaty with France and Spain, the Fox-North cabinet fell apart and the King called on Pitt to replace it. Pitt was still regarded as a reformer and so the SCI and, more importantly, Wyvill's Yorkshiremen gave him their support in the general election which he called the next spring. He gained a majority of over 100 and for good or ill the country had at last got itself a stable government. But even with such a backing, Pitt was defeated in his second attempt (in 1785) to get a parliamentary reform bill through the Commons – though it had again been a very moderate measure, intended as payment for all those Wyvill votes.

The failure of such a feeble Bill dashed the hopes of many of the reformers. Wyvill's Yorkshire movement withered away, its disappearance accelerated by the ending of the American war which had always been their main impetus for reform – taxes would now fall, the gentlemen thought, and trade would revive. SCI membership suffered too: its membership continued to drop and even those who remained seemed to lose their sense of direction – parliamentary reform took second place to involvement in the anti-slavery movement, and to other campaigns, such as those for lazaeretti (hospitals for the poor), or against impressment for the navy, or campaigns to halt the increasing use of the military to protect property, the building of barracks in London and the proposed formation of a London police force.

Some of these measures were in response to the trauma of the Gordon Riots, but for the SCI the prospect of an oppressive militarism trampling on their liberties was an even greater menace. They were inspired by an idealism embedded in past glories and future utopias. Not for them the Yorkshiremen's hard-nosed grumbles about taxes. Nor were they greatly concerned to alleviate the privations that working people were enduring. Cartwright, for instance, when he bought an estate in Lincolnshire, discovered that the woad-workers were in the habit of moving from one farm to another in pursuit of higher wages, and he had no scruples about promoting an agreement with other growers to fix the level of wages (and, incidentally, prices). His niece cheerfully describes this as 'a friendly union', for the 'mutual advantage' of the woad-producers: she applauds her uncle's increased profits, overlooking, or simply unaware of, the fact that the increased profits were a direct result of depressed conditions for the workers.

Such actions would not have disturbed the membership of the SCI, which came exclusively from the gentry and from intellectuals whose outlook did not include an empathy with the labouring poor. The Dissenters, who were well represented in the SCI, might even have regarded poverty as a form of moral deficiency; if the poor were admitted into the chapels their place was at the back of the congregation, and they were certainly not allowed a voice in the Meeting's affairs – the obduracy of the Elders of Hardy's chapel when he was canvassing for a new minister stemmed from this attitude. They could not allow him, a mere cobbler, such presumption.

The parliamentary reforms for which the SCI campaigned were not intended to disturb the social order. As for the Society's founder, Cartwright's niece explained his views thus:

> It has been often urged, as an argument against universal suffrage, that it would lead to the admission of persons into the House of Commons drawn from the lowest classes of society, whose want of education would render them unfit to associate with gentlemen. Major C. always considered this objection as fallacious; his experience of the lower orders led him to remark that they preferred confiding their interests to persons of more consideration than themselves, and that they generally evinced a jealous dislike to raise those of their own standing in society to stations of importance.

This patrician attitude to the labouring classes was widely shared by those who could afford to subscribe to the SCI. But there were exceptions. One prominent member, Thomas Brand Hollis, had become acquainted with Thomas Hardy, probably during the animated discussions in the cobbler's shop about the iniquities of the American war. They had continued their conversations in a nearby tavern. At this time Hardy found it difficult to accept that his King and country were capable of such unjust and oppressive actions towards the American colonists as those which Hollis denounced. But he was diffident in the debate, feeling himself but poorly informed and, as he listened to Hollis' well-marshalled arguments, he began to realise the naivety of his own assumptions. Hollis, however, discerned a thoughtful, if ill-educated, mind in this earnest young artisan, and into those large, toil-skilled hands he put a book – Dr Price's *Observations on the Nature of Civil Liberty.* It was not an easy read, but in the following weeks Hardy spent his evening hours studying the careful arguments which Price assembled. The effect was to totally change his outlook, to give him a political, philosophical orientation that was to inform his actions for the rest of his life. In his own words: 'He saw that it was not only necessary for the happiness of the trans-atlantic patriots themselves, that the struggle should terminate in their favour; but that even the future happiness of the whole human race was concerned in the event'.

Illustration 1: John Cartwright c 1780

13

The London Revolution Society had been founded in the early years of the eighteenth century to commemorate the 'Glorious Revolution' of 1688. Just how glorious this was, and whether it could properly be called a revolution, is doubtful. The civil war earlier in the seventeenth century had more of the flavour of a revolution, with its bloody battles culminating in the execution of the King, the transfer of power to a military dictator, and the imposition of quite new political and religious values. But the counter-revolution followed soon after the death of Cromwell. The Stuarts were restored to their throne and the Catholic James II climbed onto it in 1685.

The 'revolution' came about because the aristocracy wanted to get out from under the thumb of the King, and to rescue the country from Papist influence. They looked to William of Orange over in Holland, married to James's eldest daughter Mary, who had been the heir-presumptive until James had acquired a son. The birth of a new heir had upset William's plans to enlist the resources of England in his struggle against the French. He therefore welcomed an invitation (he may indeed have engineered it) from a group of peers and bishops to 'visit' their country, incidentally bringing an army with him. The 'Protestant winds' took his fleet down the Channel while sending the English fleet into the coast of Norfolk. So William landed unmolested at Torbay, and was greeted by bonfires and fireworks, though only because it happened to be November 5th! From Devon he progressed towards London. Elsewhere – in Cheshire, York and Nottingham – there were successful uprisings. There were desertions from King James's army and soon he thought it expedient to remove himself and his family to France, where first his son (the Old Pretender), and then his grandson (the Young Pretender, Bonnie Prince Charlie), grew up, to make abortive attempts to regain the abandoned throne at roughly thirty-year intervals.

William seemed to have cleared the board; Mary came over to join her husband and to claim her father's vacated throne. But their hosts were wary – the last fifty years had taught them much about kings and queens. A period of negotiation followed which ended in the acceptance by William and Mary of the Declaration of Rights. In return for this a second throne was found and husband and wife were installed as joint monarchs. The Declaration of Rights was not as high-minded an instrument as its name might suggest: it ensured that no Catholic, or spouse of a Catholic, could occupy the throne; it transferred the right to raise and keep an army from King to Parliament; it removed the Courts of Law, at least theoretically, from political interference and established the right to trial by jury; it declared Parliament's right to free debate, free elections and regular meetings; it established the right of subjects to petition the king. But Parliament did now have the upper hand. It controlled the purse-strings, and to William's chagrin it refused him a permanent income, making revenues dependent on the good behaviour of his government. It further ensured its independence by means of the Triennial Act which required a new Parliament to be elected at least every three years. But the power that the Crown was undoubtedly losing was not being given to 'the people': it was given to a parliament which represented solely the interests of the land-owning nobility and the increasingly influential City bankers.

Nevertheless the feeling was produced that arbitrary power had been ousted, and it was this that came to be known as the 'Glorious Revolution', and was celebrated annually by the London Revolution Society. The gloss wore thin and the celebrations lapsed after some years. The Society was reconstituted as a sort of social club for Protestant Dissenters meeting weekly at the Crown and Anchor. As the years went by the membership widened to include men from the Established Church and other persons of 'rank and consequence', but the Dissenting presence was still dominant, and the religious service which preceded the revived annual dinners was always held in the Old Jewry meeting house, with a dissenting minister preaching.[12]

So it was when the centenary of the so-called revolution was celebrated. Lord Stanhope presided. The original standard flown by William III at his Torbay landing was borne in procession, and the 300-odd members feasted themselves, drinking no less than forty-one toasts. After the dinner there were still those sober enough to propose a declaration of the Society's principles:

—That all civil and political authority is derived from the people.
—That the abuse of power justifies resistance.
—That the right of private judgement, liberty of conscience, trial by jury, freedom of the press and freedom of election ought ever to be held sacred and inviolable.

The preacher at the service which preceded this merry occasion was the Unitarian Minister Dr Andrew Kippis. Though he was a well-respected thinker in his own right, historians now often refer to him as William Godwin's tutor at the Hoxton Dissenting Academy. And Godwin himself, who was present to hear his old tutor, is apt to be known as Shelley's father-in-law, as Mary Wollstonecraft's husband, or as the father of Mary Shelley, creator of Frankenstein ... and only after all this he may be referred to as the first anarchist, the author of *An Enquiry concerning Political Justice*. In 1788 he was of course not yet any of these things.

The Centenary was celebrated not only by the Lords and Lawyers, Doctors and Reverends of the Revolution Society but in the taverns and on the streets all over London. The Tories stood aloof, of course. *The Times* of 4 November 1788 had warned somewhat sourly:

> The Anniversary of the Revolution will be celebrated in a very general manner tomorrow; and as much riot and drunkenness is the unhappy consequence of such popular occasions, the Magistrates cannot be too attentive in properly distributing constables ... All bonfires, squibs and crackers should be interdicted tomorrow...

The article ended with a plea that in place of these drunken celebrations there should be 'a day of supplication to the Almighty to restore the health of our present Sovereign'.

The health of this present sovereign, George III, had begun to deteriorate in October of the previous year when he suffered excruciating stomach pains. His doctor, Sir George Baker, attributed this to his not having changed out of his wet stockings after walking on the lawns at Windsor, and prescribed castor oil and senna; and then laudanum when the pains continued. Within a few days His Majesty was feverish, his feet were swollen, his urine brown and his stomach pains still so intense that he could only double himself up. Even so, he tried to continue with the affairs of state until, when writing to his Prime Minister, he found himself making silly mistakes, repeating himself and hardly able to control his writing. He concluded the letter: 'I am afraid, Mr Pitt, I am not quite in a situation to write at present'.

As the days passed the King's behaviour became increasingly strange. That he should rail at his doctor was perhaps not so unreasonable except that his fury lasted for all of three hours. Fanny Burney, the novelist who was then a lady-in-waiting to the Queen, recorded in her diary that she found the King one evening speaking with 'a rapidity, a hoarseness of voice, a volubility, an earnestness – a vehemence, rather' which startled her 'inexpressibly'. And at a private concert (music had usually soothed him) he talked continuously and almost incoherently, all the while rising and re-seating himself in evident agitation. Then at dinner on November 5th the King grew more and more disturbed until finally he rose in a wild fury, strode around the table to the Prince of Wales whom he dragged from his seat, hurling him violently against the wall. Again, the target of his anger was not entirely undeserving of it, but the incident convinced Sir George Baker that the King was subject to an entire 'alienation of mind', and proceeded to draw off pints of the royal blood.

But the symptoms continued unabated. The patient became alarmingly emaciated (mirrors were covered lest he should be distressed by his own reflection). He suffered mental delusions and his behaviour became increasingly bizarre. In short, the King was mad. 'Rex noster insanit', declared Dr Warren, a second, sterner doctor who had poor George moved to Kew and who instituted a punishing regime, strapping the King into a specially made chair or putting him in a straitjacket when he was obstreperous, and dosing him with an even more unsavoury assortment of nostrums.

Medical opinion nowadays diagnoses the trouble as an unfriendly bequest from the Stuarts to the House of Hanover: George III's great-grandmother was the daughter of James I, and it is thought that she carried a gene which passed on a metabolic disorder – endemic in the Stuarts – known as porphyria; George was the unfortunate descendant in whom this gene became active. But the doctors who attended him knew nothing of this and, not surprisingly, they could not agree on a prognosis: some thought he was dying, others that he had fallen incurably insane, while yet others were convinced that he had some quite temporary malady. So their bulletins were either non-committal or self-contradictory, producing fertile ground for rumour and speculation.

A similar confusion plagued the politicians, but it became apparent that the country could not continue indefinitely with a Head of State in a straitjacket. It would be necessary to appoint a Regent and this would have to be the heir-apparent, the Prince of Wales. This young man was a notorious rake whose gambling and carousing and womanising had long provided newspaper editors and cartoonists with titillating copy. But it was his political leanings which caused more consternation amongst the ruling Tories for he was well-known as a Whig sympathiser; in fact, Fox and Sheridan had been among his most constant drinking companions. In preparing a Regency Bill, Pitt knew that with its passing he would be out of a job. He delayed, but under furious pressure he eventually presented to Parliament a Bill which would enable the appointment of a Regent, though with quite severely restricted powers. After long and acrimonious debate this was passed in the Commons on 12 February 1789 and the Lords then took up the issue. They were, however, saved from a decision by the news that the King's health was on the mend. Before February was out the Lord Chancellor announced that the news was so favourable that 'it would be indecent to proceed further with the Bill when it might become wholly unnecessary'.

The country rejoiced: Pitt became a hero, Fox the villain and the Prince was in disgrace, almost a traitor for appearing to try to usurp his father's throne.

14

A service of thanksgiving for the King's recovery was held in St Paul's on 23 April 1789. Just three months later, however, ominous news began to come through from Paris – ominous for royal persons, that is, though for others it had a different complexion.

REVOLUTION IN FRANCE

The people are completely triumphant: Paris is now one general Scene of tumultuous Joy – Despotism is destroyed – Necker is returned ... At Night the Bells were ringing and every Appearance of Joy manifested itself thoughout the Capital. Much remains to be done: every Thing however is to be looked for from the firmness of our Citizens, the Patriotism of our native Soldiers and the Wisdom of our National Assembly.

Our Messenger ... on the road to Calais was stopped at almost every Town ... The Mob, however, everywhere obliged him to cry out *Vive le Thiers Etat!*...The Blow is therefore struck ... In every Province of this great Kingdom the Flame of Liberty has burst forth ... but before they have accomplished their End, France will be deluged with Blood.

The Revolution that has taken Place in France astonishes every Politician. That a Nation, whose Characteristic for several Centuries has been

Submission to Slavery, should have on a Sudden, in the Twinkling of an Eye, been animated with the boldest Spirit of Liberty and Patriotism, is an Event to be contemplated with Wonder.[13]

Many Englishmen, Scots and Welsh shared the 'tumultuous joy' which inflamed Paris. There was young Wordsworth, blissfully alive; there was Godwin who declared that his heart 'beat high with great swelling sentiments of Liberty'.[14] Even Cartwright was moved to shift slightly out of his usual prosaic mode: 'Degenerate must be the heart which expands not with sentiments of delight at what is now transacting in the national Assembly of France'. He was writing to the President of the Committee of Constitution in Paris; assuming that the French were modelling themselves on the incomparable British, he went on to deliver a lecture on the defects which they must avoid.

There were of course some 'degenerate hearts', which did not expand in quite this way. *The Times*, for instance, reported these events in a quite different mood:

> The relation of what Paris has been doing during the last week fills the mind with horror; and although we have seen and felt the sad effects of an unlicensed populace in our own country at the time of the dreadful conflagration in London during the riots of 1780, yet even that melancholy event was far short of the general distress which not only is felt in Paris but in the neighbourhood for many leagues around it...[15]

But for the time being these voices were not much heard. The events in France seemed to hold out new prospects for all of Europe to 'advance the general liberties of mankind', as Cartwright put it. So the Revolution Society met for their annual commemoration that year in euphoric mood. *La jour de gloire* had surely arrived. Dr Richard Price who was given the honour of preaching at the traditional Old Jewry meeting looked back on a life devoted to the cause which now seemed on the brink of triumph. 'I have lived to see a diffusion of knowledge', he said, 'which has undermined superstition and error. I have lived to see the rights of men better understood than ever; and nations panting for liberty, which seemed to have lost the idea of it. I have lived to see THIRTY MILLIONS of people, indignant and resolute, spurning at slavery, and demanding liberty with an irresistible voice; their king led in triumph, and an arbitrary monarch surrendering himself to his subjects.'

As he climbed the pulpit, this ageing, gentle, thoughtful man may have remembered his father, Rhys Prys, schoolmaster in the remote Welsh community of Cowbridge and a leading figure in the blossoming culture there, soon to make its mark by reviving the Eisteddfod, as much as a vehicle for radical propaganda as for Welsh poetry and song. Here was Richard's school of liberation. He left it early, first to study mathematics and then to become a Unitarian minister. It was his book *Observations on the nature of civil liberty*, published in 1776 in support of the American colonists, which gave Thomas Hardy his first and lasting political perspective. Price was honoured in the new American nation and later he became well-known in revolutionary circles in France: 'one of the formative minds of the century', as the philosopher Condorcet dubbed him.[16]

In fact, he was one of the first modern internationalists. The sermon that he preached on this notable occasion was subsequently published under the title *A discourse on the Love of our Country*. But it was no chauvinist effusion: he was reflecting on the nature of patriotic love for a citizen of the world. Such love, he argued, dictated the duty to ensure that, on the one hand, one's country did nothing to infringe the liberty of its citizens, and on the other, that it maintained a 'just regard to the rights of other countries'. He reminded his congregation of the three principles of the Revolution Society (p52), and pointed to some important imperfections he saw in the English revolution which they were commemorating: it had left the country with only limited religious toleration, inadequate parliamentary representation and a corrupt parliament. The example that France was setting would perhaps give an impetus to correct these injustices. 'Be encouraged', he concluded, 'all ye friends of freedom, and writers in its defence! The times are auspicious. Your labours have not been in vain. Behold kingdoms starting from sleep, breaking their fetters and claiming justice from their oppressors! Behold the light you have struck, after setting America free, reflected in France, and there kindled into a blaze that lays despotism in ashes, and warms and illuminates Europe!'

With this he sent his congregation away in good spirits for the less sober part of their celebrations, the dinner at the London Tavern that same evening. Numerous toasts were drunk, brave resolutions were passed, and Dr Price himself moved an address to the French National Assembly, congratulating them on their 'glorious example' which would 'encourage other nations to assert the inalienable rights of mankind ... to make the world free and happy'.

This was just what the conservative forces, growling in the background, had feared; and it was not long before the backlash made itself felt. Edmund Burke, no longer a partner in Fox's Whig party, was chief growler, spreading alarm about the Dissenting conspiracy which, he averred, aimed at the destruction of the constitution and of the Church. This warning was not lost on Burke's new Tory friends. One of the first effects was the defeat of a motion presented to the Commons in 1790 for the repeal of the Test and Corporation Acts (which excluded dissenters from public office). This motion had been put forward each year throughout the 1780s with gradually growing support. But now it was thrown out by a majority of three to one. And when, two days later, the SCI member Henry Flood introduced a fairly modest proposal of reform to give the vote to resident householders, the graphic declaration of Burke's friend William Windham that 'the hurricane season was no time to repair one's house' was enough to cause Flood to withdraw his motion.

But the full force Burke's hostility was felt when, in reaction to Price's address he published his book *Reflections on the Revolution in France* (see Chapter 18).

Notes

1. *Northampton Mercury*, 25 December 1775.
2. *Documents of the American Revolution*, Vol VI, p196.
3. *Northampton Mercury*, 20 February 1775.
4. *Ibid.*, 17 April 1775 (such items would have taken about 2 months to cross the Atlantic).
5. Quotations here and below from F. Cartwright, *The Life and Correspondence of John Cartwright.*
6. See Hill's essay 'The Norman Yoke', in John Saville (ed), *Democracy and the Labour Movement.* For a note about the Levellers, see chapter 23.
7. Boswell's credentials for membership rested partly on his book *Account of Corsica* which reported the island's struggle for independence, under its hero General Paoli, who had tried to inveigle Rousseau to come to Corsica as a kind of political consultant. It seems that Rousseau toyed with the idea but decided against it, not daring to put himself at the mercy of these 'semi-barbarous and ferocious people' (see his *Confessions*, Book XII). Instead, he fled to England where, alas, he did not find the natives very much more hospitable. Boswell could also have entertained the coffee-houses with

tales of Rousseau's beloved Thérèse whom he conducted across the continent to join Jean-Jacques in London, taking the opportunity to seduce her on the way – ten times in thirteen days, he boasted in his diary.

8. Alan Wharam has unearthed the record of this marriage in the registers of St Martins-in-the-Fields, Westminster (see *The Treason Trials*, p22). In his *Memoir*, Hardy does not divulge his wife's name although he was obviously devotedly attached to her.

9. *Northampton Mercury*, 11 December 1777.

10. All quotes taken from letters printed in the *Northampton Mercury*, 23 & 30 August 1779.

11. Quoted in De Castro, *The Gordon Riots*, p145.

12. The Old Jewry is a street in the City of London which had been the centre of the Jewish community until all Jews (16000 of them) had been expelled from England in 1290.

13. *Northampton Mercury*, 25 July1789.

14. Similar sentiments were felt by liberals in this century. Leonard Woolf, for instance, writes in his autobiography: 'The Russian Revolution in 1917 was a tremendous event for me and all those whose beliefs and hopes had been moulded in the revolutionary fires of liberty, equality, fraternity'. He adds however: 'The intelligent revolutionary knows, however, that all revolutions must disappoint him. There is nothing more violent than violence ... Nevertheless the destruction of the *ancien régime* in France and of the Tsarist regime in Russia was essential ... That is why, if I could return to 1789 and 1917, I would still be on the side of the revolution'. Leonard Woolf, *Beginning Again*, pp207, 215.

15. *The Times*, 20th July 1789.

16. Price's tombstone in the Bunhill Fields Burial Ground (near the City Rd entrance) stands only a few yards from that of Hardy (See chapter 44).

Part II Actions

15

Soon after his marriage Hardy was promoted to foreman in the shoe-maker's shop where he worked. The extra money enabled him to rent a terraced house giving space enough to rear the growing family. But it never grew large, for the children all died in infancy, victims of a poor diet that did not furnish the resistance to the diseases that abounded in the slums of eighteenth-century London.

A thoughtful man like Hardy could not easily accept that life should necessarily be so fraught. He had spent his early years in the Scottish countryside and knew well that the land was productive, the people industrious and intelligent. Why then was there everywhere such distress? All around him men and women trudged the dirty streets, their faces lined and yellowing. Young girls were being forced into prostitution, boys into petty crime. The men who came into his shop with leisure enough to spend their mornings gossiping were well-clothed and well-fed, while he and Lydia, for all their toil and care, had to watch their children sicken and die. The news of the uprising in France, the storming of the Bastille, the crowds marching behind the severed heads mounted on poles of their erstwhile masters, was greeted by many with hopes of similar acts of vengeance in London streets. The news stirred Hardy too, but he was a man of peace, more perceptive than many of those he lived alongside. He still remembered the drunken days of the Gordon riots at the beginning of the decade. There must be other ways.

In 1791 his personal circumstances took a more hopeful turn. He was approached by two men, a currier and a leather-cutter, who proposed that they should supply him with dressed leather and market the footwear that he should make. He left his old employer and found a house at No 9 Piccadilly, large enough to provide him with a workshop as well as accommodating his small family. It seemed the beginning of a climb into an independent way of life with growing comfort. But their hopes soon crumbled: within a couple of months Hardy's partners found themselves in financial trouble. They pulled out of the agreement and demanded immediate payment for the leather they had already supplied. Having no savings of his own, Hardy faced ruin. Fortunately he had friends ready to help, and was in fact able to continue trading and to build up a fairly profitable business. He does not tell us exactly who it was who rescued him. There are several possibilities.

A frequent visitor to the Hardy household was Lydia's brother-in-law, George Walne, but he is unlikely to have been in a position to offer financial help. One with more resources was a lodger Olhaudah Equiano, an African who had been taken into slavery, bought his freedom and after many adventures, hardships and betrayals, had accumulated a not inconsiderable wealth.[1] But he stayed with the Hardys for only a few months. Then there was Colonel Smith, an American who was in London working as secretary to his father-in-law, Ambassador John Adams, and with whom Hardy had become 'very intimate' probably after Smith had visited the cobbler's shop. He had tried to persuade Hardy to emigrate to the new continent, promising to find him a good position in that rapidly growing society.

But the friend most likely to have rescued him from financial ruin was Thomas Hollis, the man who had given him that treatise of Dr Price's which had opened his mind to an inspiring vision of civil liberties. Hollis was a rich man and Hardy's debt would have seemed a very minor difficulty to him. There were more important things for Hardy to be concerned with than mere money problems. Hollis had followed the gift of Price's book with a stream of pamphlets which the SCI were publishing (and, incidentally, distributing free) written by such men as Cartwright, Dr Jebb, Dr Price, Reverend Mr Stone, John Horne Tooke, the Duke of Richmond and others. Most of these tracts had come out in the early 1780s, but now with more time on his hands, Hardy turned to them again for help in solving the conundrum that haunted him: why did the riches of Britain leave the majority of its citizens in such distressing poverty? 'It required no extraordinary penetration,' he wrote, 'once the enquiry was begun, to be able to trace it to the corrupt practices of men falsely calling themselves representatives of the people, but who were, in fact, selected by comparatively few influential individuals who preferred their own particular aggrandisement to the general interest of the community.'

This conclusion was in line with, and of course informed by, the SCI writings which he was studying, but the route he trod was not theirs. The gentlemen of the SCI were in no way interested in the travails of working people: they were concerned with the political and ethical aspects of the loss of liberty which, they argued, resulted from a corrupt and unrepresentative parliament. The pamphlets which Hardy found especially useful – Thomas Day's *British and Foreign History*, the Duke of Richmond's *Letter to Col. Sharman*, and John Cartwright's *Give us our Rights* – were all based on the idea that men's liberty was God-given and had been denied ever since the days of King Henry VI. The reforms they wanted – annual parliaments, universal male suffrage, numerically equalised constituencies – were intended to restore that freedom; they were not so much concerned with putting bread into hungry mouths.

Of these three publications, it was Richmond's that came later to have the greatest significance by putting the stamp of respectability on Hardy's schemes – for the Duke was of royal, if bastard, descent. His *Letter* was written in response to an appeal from a group of Irish 'Volunteers' (akin to the English militia) who had met to discuss the possible reform of the Irish parliament which had been set up in 1782 in the likeness (warts and all) of the English model. Among the warts were all the defects of representation which the English reformers were labouring to correct – the very restricted suffrage, rotten boroughs, unequal constituencies, etc. Lt-Col Sharman had been deputed to ask advice of the Duke of Richmond, and must have been gratified to receive such a full reply.

It was the Duke of Richmond's Bill to reform the English parliament that was being debated in the Upper House while Lord Gordon's rioters seethed outside in 1780. The Bill was, of course, thrown out, but Richmond did not abandon his ideas. His letter to Sharman is in effect a lengthy rationale of the rejected Bill, which would have put into effect most of what Cartwright had argued for in *Take your Choice*. Most contentious perhaps was the idea of universal suffrage (men only, of course). The usual assumption was that only those who 'had a stake' in the country (i.e. owned property and paid taxes) should be given the vote; but 'I know of no man,' Richmond wrote, 'let him be ever so poor, who, in his consumption of food and use of raiment, does not pay taxes, and I would wish to encourage an enthusiasm for his country in the breast of every subject, by giving him his just share in its government.' With universal suffrage 'bribery must entirely cease ... The numbers to be bought would be infinitely too great for any purse.

Besides annual parliaments, by their frequency, and by their shortness, would doubly operate in preventing corruption.' But the Duke still respected the traditional constitution: 'I am not for a democrat, any more than for an aristocratic, or a monarchic, government solely: I am for that admirable mixture of the three.' He agreed with Sharman in wishing 'to restore to the Crown its original splendour, to nobility its ancient privileges, and to the nation at large its inherent rights', though he was against 'restoring the negative of the Crown ... it appears to me preposterous that the will of one man should for ever obstruct every regulation which all the rest of the nation may think necessary'.

So Hardy sat many an evening, reading and cogitating on what should be done. Sometimes Lydia sat with him, sewing. Sometimes George, her brother-in-law, would call and Thomas would tell him about what he had been reading. Some evenings Thomas Hollis would come and they would discuss the latest news from France, perhaps, or Burke's book *Reflections on the Revolution in France*, or one or other of the numerous pamphlets which that book had provoked, among them Tom Paine's *Rights of Man* which was causing a new sensation. Lydia might listen to the talk; but she would keep her silence, knowing it was men's talk. (This was a year before Mary Wollstonecraft's *Vindication of the Rights of Women* appeared). Not that Lydia would have read it, nor the men been inclined to discuss it, as in any case 'Votes for women' was not really on the eighteenth century agenda. Wollstonecraft made scant reference to it in her *Vindication*. She did write somewhat apologetically ' I may excite laughter..for I really think that women ought to have representatives': and then dismissed the subject by adding, 'But as the whole system of representation is now, in this country, only a convenient handle for despotism, they need not complain for they are as well represented as a numerous class of hard-working mechanics.'[2]

Hollis told Hardy about the Revolution Society's Dinner – the 101st celebration of the 'Glorious Revolution'. Dr Price had been there, ailing, but not so much as to prevent him from climbing onto the table to propose the daring toast: 'The Parliament of Britain – may it become a National Assembly'. This was the title of the French revolutionary parliament which was supposed to be representative of the whole nation in a way that could not be claimed for the House of Commons.

Hollis also brought Hardy a copy of Price's most recently published booklet *Discourse on the Love of Our Country*, and it was here that Hardy found the idea of forming societies 'throughout the Kingdom ...

to maintain a correspondence with each other and to form a union of the true friends of public liberty'. Could there be such a society started in London, he wondered, a society aimed at the radical reform of parliament. A society for all those in London who were now denied a vote, open to all classes of men, a society to inspire and join with others elsewhere. 'For it is as clear as a mathematical axiom that the whole Mass of people are unrepresented or misrepresented'.

He sat late staring into the dying embers in the grate, constructing the Society in his mind. How would it function? What rules would be necessary? How should it make its influence felt? To publish tracts like the SCI? But could its members find the money to do this? And what should it be called? He looked again at Price's suggestions, a country-wide network of societies 'to maintain a correspondence with each other'. It should be called a corresponding society then. The London Corresponding Society of the Unrepresented Part of the People of Great Britain.

16

A NOTE ABOUT PARLIAMENTARY REPRESENTATION

Twenty-two years after the 'glorious revolution', when Queen Anne had replaced William III (who had ruled alone for eight years after Mary's death), an Act was passed which determined the way in which members were to be elected to parliament throughout the eighteenth century. As much as anything it demonstrated the limitations of the 1688 'revolution': power was transferred in some significant ways from the sovereign to parliament, but it was to be a parliament of property, not a parliament of the people.

There were to be 558 members of Parliament. These would represent the 122 County constituencies (80 of England, 12 of Wales and 30 of Scotland) and 230 Borough constituencies. Most constituencies would return two or more members. The men in County constituencies qualified to vote if they held freehold property yielding at least 40 shillings per annum. It has been estimated that about one-fifth of all the men living in these areas would have qualified on this basis. But the size of the constituencies varied enormously. Yorkshire, for instance, had some 20,000 voters, while the other counties had electorates ranging from only 800 to 8000.

The other members were elected by the Boroughs, of which there were 215 in England and Wales and 15 in Scotland. These boroughs had differing franchise qualifications, and had acquired quaint names accordingly: in some (the pot wallopers) you could vote if you were a male householder not on poor relief; in others (scot-and-lot boroughs) you had to be a householder paying poor rates. Or perhaps you lived in a freeman borough where you could vote only if you had earned the freedom of the borough – in London this limited the franchise to members of the liveried companies. In the burbage boroughs you did not even have to live there – the right to vote depended on the owner-ship of certain properties. And in the corporation boroughs voting was limited to members of the governing body.

These varying rules gave rise to even greater anomalies in voting ratios than in the Shires. Most notorious were those like Old Sarum and Gatten where there were no residents at all, but for which there were seven and two voters respectively! These came to be known as 'rotten boroughs' (for obvious reasons), or 'pocket' boroughs, because they were in the pockets of the members of the aristocracy who owned the land on which they were situated.

In Cornwall there were 21 boroughs (corporation towns) which between them sent 42 men to Parliament on the votes of 453 electors. Most of these boroughs dated from the time of Queen Elizabeth who had created them to secure her ascendancy in Parliament. Of these 453 Cornish voters, 60 lived in St Ives, the largest electorate; two of the other boroughs had 50 voters each; and the rest had 30 or less, with five of them down to single figures. The lowest was Helston, with just 3 voters. By contrast, the fast-growing towns in the North and the Midlands – Birmingham, Leeds, Manchester, Sheffield, Wolverhampton – had not a single representative in Parliament.

The term 'representative' seems a doubtful description in view of these figures. In their first communication to the public the London Corresponding Society commented: 'Upon the whole it appears that 257 supposed Representatives of the People, making a Majority of the House of Commons, are returned by a Number of Voters not exceed-ing the thousandth part of the Nation'.

The 1710 Act decreed elections every three years, but in 1716 parlia-ment decided it should have a life of up to seven years and it was not until 1784 that a parliament lasted less than six years. And even when general elections were called there were contests in by no means all the constituencies: it was quite usual to arrange that there were no more candidates in a borough than there were seats. Obviously this saved a lot of bother – and expense, since persuading people to vote for you usually involved costly 'treats'.

If the franchise was restricted, even more so was the eligibility for election. Only those who were deemed to 'have a stake' in the country were allowed to stand for parliament, and having a stake meant being a man of property – for this was a parliament of property. Membership of the Commons was thus virtually restricted to the sons of Peers, to members of the military and legal professions, and to the owners of big businesses – bankers, manufacturers, overseas traders and the like.

17

Having formulated his idea of a 'Corresponding Society', Hardy set about working out details of how it should operate – how it would recruit members, how it would finance itself, what the rules of the Society should be, and so on. He wrote his ideas down and in a few days he tested them out on three of his closest friends – his wife's brother-in-law George Walne, Robert Boyd who was the landlord of The Bell, a tavern in Exeter Street off the Strand, and William Gow, a young watchmaker. Walne, of course, already had a good inkling of the way Hardy was thinking, but to Boyd and Gow the ideas were new and startling. They needed no convincing that the conditions of life were hard and that as things stood they were powerless to improve their lot. But how would this 'club' help?

'Is it a revolution you're thinking of, like the Frenchies?' William Gow asked. They had to force a change, Hardy explained, but not by cutting people's heads off. They had to persuade people that Parliament is theirs and should be making laws to help them. And when they had persuaded enough people, the men in Parliament would *have* to change. As they talked, Hardy's friends began to understand his vision of a host of people throughout the country waking from their despair and clamouring for the change that would bring relief from the oppression. They agreed to meet the following week, each bringing a friend. Robert Boyd offered to find a room at the Bell.

Nine men met together on the next Monday evening, 23 January 1792. They supped on bread and cheese and porter, talking of the day, nine, ten hours work in cold rooms most of them, for a few shillings pay that would barely feed their families let alone pay the rent, buy a few rags to clothe their growing children. It was familiar talk, familiar worries. They needed more pay, but if they asked for it they would be told there were plenty of men eager to take their place. Low wages were better than no wages.

But then the talk took an unfamiliar turn. Quietly Hardy began to tell them of the reading he had done over the last few months. They were powerless, he said, because they were victims of law-makers on whom they had no influence, against whom they had no appeal. He read them a passage from Cartwright's *Give us our rights*. First the kings of England, foreign kings, had stolen the power that belonged to the people, stripped them of their freedoms, made slaves of free men. The Glorious Revolution, a hundred years old, had wrested back that power to put it in the hands of Parliament. This was supposed to be a forum of the people, but the people had no part in it. Hardy pulled some figures from the table in Cartwright's book which demonstrated the farcical state of the so-called representation. 'Three men in Helston can vote two men to represent them in Parliament. You know where Helston is?' None had heard of Helston. 'Two members of Parliament are voted in by six men in Camelford. Another six in St Germains vote in another two Members. Where are these places? They're all in Cornwall. Cornwall has 42 Members of Parliament put there by a mere 450 voters. And how many members represent the two hundred thousand souls in Manchester? None. No members for Sheffield. None for Birmingham.

His eight listeners heard all this in astonished silence. Hardy read parts of the Duke of Richmond's *Letter to Col. Sharman*, which spelled out the reforms of parliament that were needed; and then he turned back to Cartwright: 'I would to God that people would cease to be victims of self-delusions ... It is THEMSELVES that must seek a cure ... To be a MAN is a title to Liberty; and he who doth not assert it deserves not the name of a MAN!'

Hardy then urged his plans to form a club which would aim to study these matters, to inform people, and to link up with other such clubs in various parts of the country, so that a body of opinion would grow that would have the weight to change things. He was not a great orator, but this small gathering could hear his sincerity and they realised that he had given more thought to the subject than any of them had done. They were moved by his quiet, determined insistence that change was possible. All but one of the men (and he kept quiet at this stage) were convinced. They began to exchange ideas about what the new club should be called. The Patriotic Club? The Reformation Society? The Constitutional Society? It was only when Hardy produced the membership cards on which he had put a provisional title that everyone agreed that this was exactly right: The London Corresponding Society.

Hardy then outlined the organisation that would be necessary. The Society would need funds to pay for the cost of correspondence and of any printing that they might decide on in the future. He proposed that each member should pay one penny each week, which was a usual arrangement for journeymen's clubs, friendly societies, and the like. This was now agreed without objection. He then explained that they would need to appoint a Treasurer and a Secretary. Looking around the room it seemed to the others that none but Hardy was fit for these offices. 'They stumbled at the threshold,' he wrote later. 'Two very important offices filled by one person.'

However, at the time he accepted both roles and thereupon produced the book that he had ruled up, asking them to enter their names and pay him their first week's subscription. In return he gave them each a membership card. Only the one doubter refrained, saying that he wanted to think about it before committing himself.

They arranged to meet again on the following Monday and Hardy walked home through the moonlit streets, filled with satisfaction at the evening's proceedings. His thoughts were perhaps interrupted along the way by a woman's screams, or a man's angry drunken shouts from one of the dark houses, sounds of the wretchedness that he aimed to relieve. Back home, as Lydia looked up from her sewing, Thomas declared 'We have founded the London Corresponding Society!', slamming down on the table the subscriptions he had collected. 'There! With those eight pennies we are going to reform the House of Commons!' Lydia, seeing her husband's face, usually so solemn, now alight with his vision, kept her forebodings to herself.

The eight pennies soon began to grow. At the second meeting eight new members were enrolled (including the man who had hesitated the previous week). In the third week the membership grew to twenty-five so that the treasurer found himself with four shillings and a penny – a mighty sum, as he later recalled. It was an encouraging beginning though Hardy's ambition encompassed a far greater society than this. They started laying down the rules that would govern their proceedings. They would meet every Monday evening. At each meeting they would appoint a chairman for the following week. The Secretary was to record the minutes of each meeting. The number of members was to be unlimited. Any man over 20 years of age who was introduced by an existing member would be eligible to join.

The members of the new London Corresponding Society (LCS) had set their hands to the reform of the nation's parliament, no less. Yet as they looked at themselves, twenty-five working-men seated round a bare wooden table in an ill-lit room, many of them must have wondered how they could hope to change the ways of those great gentlemen, those Lords and Dukes, whom none of them had ever seen, let alone met and talked to. And even if their demand for the vote was granted, what difference would it make? Would it bring down the price of bread? Would they be paid higher wages because they had a vote to cast every seven years? Perhaps only Hardy had conviction and vision enough to see these mountains climbed, and the promised land beyond. But he did not harangue them. He listened.

Before they dispersed they agreed on three questions to be discussed at their next meeting:

—Is there any necessity for a reformation of the present State of Representation in the British House of Commons?

—Would there be any Utility in a parliamentary reform? – or in other words – Are there any just grounds to believe that a reformation of parliament will be of any essential service to the Nation?

—Have we who are Tradesmen, Shopkeepers and mechanicks any right to seek to obtain a parliamentary reform?

Hardy wrote out these questions in the minute-book. Then, having appointed next week's chairman, the twenty-five men returned to their several homes, some elated, many with doubts.

THOMAS HARDY.

Illustration 2: Thomas Hardy c. 1794

18

The discussion of these three questions occupied the members of the LCS for all five evenings of the following week. While they are thus engaged we shall take the opportunity to introduce a couple of characters who are to play important parts in this story.

The first, Tom Paine, is well-known to this day, and his most influential book, *The Rights of Man*, is still in print two centuries later. He was born in 1737, the son of a Quaker artisan, and started his working life in his father's trade as a corset-maker. He left this to become first a teacher then a shopkeeper, and finally a collector of excise duty. In 1774 he emigrated to America and within two years he had set the colonists agog with a book that he called *Common Sense* in which he advocated independence for the colonies and the establishment of a Republic of America – this at a time when few colonists, though they chafed under British rule, had dared to think in such radical terms. His writing was so persuasive that the ideas quickly took root and Paine found himself in the forefront of the revolutionary thrust. He was involved in the formulation of the Declaration of Independence and was among those, Washington, Jefferson, Madison, Franklin, and others, who planned the constitution of the new nation.

The war of independence having been won, and with it pretty well all that Paine had argued for, he returned to Europe in 1787. He went to France first where, curiously, he sought to sell his design of a single-span iron bridge, which had become his new obsession. But France was brewing its own revolution, and Paine was of more interest as the author of *Common Sense* than as the designer of bridges, however advanced. He found himself greeted as something of a celebrity, particularly by his friend Jefferson, who was the American Ambassador at Versailles, and by Lafayette, who had fought in America, and was now a leader of the 'Patriots' challenging the power of the King.

Thus Paine became involved in another nation's political upheaval. But he was still preoccupied with his bridge and soon returned to England, intending at least to get models made. Here again his reputation had preceded him, and inevitably he was drawn into the political vortex. He became involved with the Whig hierarchy, with Fox, Sheridan and Burke who had supported the American colonists and were now interested to hear about the rumblings in France.

Then came the storming of the Bastille, and a few months later Paine was back in Paris though for only a short while. When he returned to England he carried in his baggage the key to the Bastille, which Lafayette had entrusted to him as a gift for George Washington, now President of America. In sending it, Paine enclosed a personal token of half-a-dozen razors 'manufactured from the cast-steel works where the [model of the] Bridge was constructed' (!)

Soon after Paine's return to London Edmund Burke's book *Reflections on the Revolution in France* appeared. This was a powerful denunciation of the revolution in which other Whigs at that time were rejoicing. It destroyed Burke's position in the Whig leadership and it put an end to the friendship between Burke and Paine. Paine immediately took up his pen and within a little over four months his response, the first part of *The Rights of Man*, was on the streets.

Burke's objective had been to warn the country of the danger of the 'false philosophy' that fired the French Revolution spreading across Europe and even, he thought, erupting here at home. By 'the country' he meant the ruling classes of course – the rest he referred to as 'the swinish multitude', a give-away phrase that was to haunt him in the coming years of controversy. His book was written in the classical style (though with unusually emotive passages) that only educated gentlemen would have appreciated. Paine, on the other hand, addressed 'the people' – that is, the lower middle classes and that part of the working class which was literate: in place of literary elegance and classical allusions he used a more direct style, an 'intellectual vernacular prose' Olivia Smith calls it,[3] coloured with memorable images. And to such great effect that no less than 200,000 copies of *The Rights of Man* were sold in its first year.[4] In fact, although Burke had hoped to head off dangerous ideas, his book had exactly the opposite effect by provoking Paine's persuasive polemic.[5]

Burke had argued that the settlement of 1688 had fixed 'to the end of time' the powers of the monarchy, of the hereditary aristocracy and of Parliament, and that no one had the right to alter this. Paine was scathing: 'Mr Burke is contending for the authority of the dead over the rights and freedom of the living ... Every age and generation must be as free to act for itself as the ages and generations that preceded it. The vanity and presumption of governing beyond the grave is the most insolent and ridiculous of all tyrannies.' As for Burke's account of the events in Paris, Paine refuted this in detail, and with the advantage of a certain amount of first-hand knowledge. He ridiculed Burke's lamentations for the indignities suffered by the King and Queen of France (still in possession of their heads at that time), pointing to the greater suffering that the people of France had endured – 'he pities the plumage but forgets the dying bird'. Burke's criticisms of the National Assembly and their new Constitution were gratuitously 'insulting'. 'I readily perceive the reason why Mr Burke declined going into the comparison between the English and French constitutions, because he could not but perceive ... that no such thing as a constitution existed on his side of the question.'

The second part of *The Rights of Man* appeared eleven months later. In this, Paine described what he hoped a new republic would achieve. It took a hundred and fifty years before his vision for a welfare society was enacted – maternity grants, married couple's allowances, child allowances, education grants, old-age pensions. The British Republic and a written constitution is not yet with us.

The Rights of Man became the bible for many, though not all, of the radical reformers. There were those who were embarrassed, particularly by Paine's republicanism. Major Cartwright, for instance (to quote his niece), 'never wished in his own country to interfere with its ancient institutions', only to reform them. The government, though, were seriously alarmed, especially when a cheap edition of the book came out. Booksellers who dared to handle it were liable to find themselves in prison and Paine himself was forced to flee the country to avoid prosecution.

The second man to be introduced here was generally known as John Horne Tooke. His father was plain Mr Horne, a poultry dealer but, ambitious for his son, he scraped together money enough to send his son to Eton and thence to Cambridge where John graduated and was later ordained. He followed his father's wishes in serving conscientiously as a clergyman for eleven years but his real interests were in politics and the law. He supported Wilkes in that maverick's long struggle with the establishment; and he became embroiled in a number of legal cases, including one concerning the estate of his friend William Tooke (whose name he later added to his own). His provocative tactics on this occasion resulted in his being convicted of seditious libel and earned him a year in gaol. All of this aroused such antagonism amongst the legal hierarchy that when he applied to be called to bar he was refused.

However he was by now wealthy enough to settle in Wimbledon, where he devoted himself to writing a book, *Diversions of Purley* (about his long-time hobby of philology), to sundry political forays, and to entertaining his friends. The latter he did notably with regular Sunday dinners which became famous as gatherings of radical reformers and as a stage for Horne Tooke's conversational arts. Indeed it was this which came to be regarded as his most enviable talent and, though he frequently exercised it to the discomfiture of his many of his guests, the dinner parties continued to be well-attended social events.

In commenting on this William Hazlitt (not a great admirer of Horne Tooke) quotes one witness as saying: 'I was never in his company without being delighted or surprised, or without feeling the conversation of every other person to be flat in comparison. But I do not recollect having ever heard him make a remark that struck me as a sound or true one, or that he himself appeared to think so.' He delighted in the clash of controversy and, in the fashion of a lawyer, would argue any case that presented itself.

This characteristic spilled over, according to Hazlitt, into his political interventions. 'It was his delight to make mischief ... Provided he could say a clever or a spiteful thing, he did not care whether it served or injured the cause.' So although he allied himself with the reformist movement (he became an active member of the Society for Constitutional Information and of Friends of the People), he was not an altogether reliable ally. In fact, in many ways his pedantry and his elitist leanings seem to contradict his overt radicalism. But perhaps this stemmed from a consciousness of his family origins, which he had always felt necessary to disguise in the aristocratic company into which he was thrust at Eton and Cambridge. And this may account for his wanting to 'get off at Hounslow rather than going all the way to Windsor' – a metaphor he used repeatedly to signify that he favoured a reform of parliament but not a Painite republic. In this he was with Cartwright but they disagreed on the question of a universal suffrage; Horne Tooke proposed a £2-rate-paying qualification (which would have excluded most working men).

In debate, it may have been true that, as Hazlitt wrote: 'He would rather be against himself than for anybody else'; but he was capable of apparently unselfish actions in giving help to those who seemed to need it, whether it was the widow of a murdered man, or two weavers condemned to death for rioting, the politician Wilkes or his friend

Tooke, or the working men struggling to set up reform societies in London and elsewhere. It was this that was to land him in the Tower of London on a charge of High Treason.

19

The founder members of the London Corresponding Society debated all week the three questions they had set themselves until they finally agreed to answer Yes, Yes and Yes. It was of course the debate rather than the answers that was significant. The questions were a little later translated into three other questions to which new members were expected to reply in the Affirmative:

1) Are you convinced that the parliamentary Representation of this Country is at present inadequate and imperfect?

2) Are you thoroughly persuaded that the welfare of these kingdoms requires that every person of Adult years in possession of his reason and not incapacitated by crimes should have a vote for a member of parliament?

3) Will you endeavour by all justifiable means to promote such reformation in parliament?

Subsequently, the members, now numbering about fifty, were considerably surprised and heartened by Hardy's announcement that he had opened a correspondence with a group in 'a distant part of the country' calling itself the Sheffield Society for Constitutional Information. They were surprised because they had had no idea that another such society of working men existed elsewhere, and were encouraged to learn that it had begun to act in the same way as themselves. 'It animated them with additional ardour', Hardy remarked in his *Memoir*. In fact the Sheffield Society had started before the LCS – in November 1791 – and by the time Hardy, having seen mention of them in a newspaper, wrote to ask their advice their membership had reached 2000. They recommended the Society for Constitutional Information in London, and Horne Tooke in particular, who 'will be a true Friend and advocate of our Cause'. They also told Hardy that they divided themselves into groups of ten, each of these 'tythings' sending a delegate to their monthly meeting.

This arrangement was one that the LCS soon adopted. As soon as a group reached 60 members it was to divide into six groups by neighbourhood, and each group, or 'Division', was to elect a delegate to attend the meetings of what came to be called the General Committee every Thursday evening. The weekly meetings of the Divisions were the occasions when members heard about, and could contribute to, the business of the Society and some at least of the Divisions developed into important educative experiences for the members. 'I met with many inquisitive clever upright men,' writes Francis Place in his *Autobiography*. 'We had Sunday evening parties at the residences of those who could accommodate a number of persons. At these meetings we had readings, conversations, and discussions.' The readings were from books which would be passed around those members who chose to subscribe to their purchase. Place describes how at the Sunday meetings the chairman (each member taking the chair in rotation) would read a passage which would then be discussed. After two further readings and discussions 'there was a general discussion. No one was allowed to speak more than once during the reading. The same rule was observed in the general discussion, no one could speak a second time until every one who chose had spoken once'. These procedures were typical of the disciplined way in which the Society's business was conducted: 'eating – drinking – & smoaking were forbidden either in a division or in a committee. No man in liquor was permitted to remain in any division or committee, and habitual drunkenness was sufficient cause for expulsion.'

Soon after the Society's foundation the members were joined by two men who were not of their own class. One was Lord Daer, a radical peer, a friend of Tom Paine, and immediately there was a move to elect him chairman. However, Hardy objected to this: the members had to learn to rely on themselves, he argued, and they should resist the temptation to hand the reins to someone just because that person was a Nobleman. The move was quashed. Likewise, when Lord Daer offered to subscribe more than the required one penny a week, Hardy refused: 'we had money sufficient for all necessary purposes Viz for printing, postage of letters, and stationery.'

The other unusual new member was one Maurice Margarot. He was an educated man, clever, thrusting, widely travelled, the manager of a flourishing wine business in Marylebone. He was very soon elected to the chair of the newly formed general committee, apparently with no objection from Hardy.

One of the first tasks which the committee set itself was to prepare an 'Address to the Nation' which was to be the first public announcement of the Society's existence. They had some difficulty with this: several members prepared drafts but none was approved at their next meeting. 'We are full of self-importance,' Hardy confided to Horne Tooke, whom he had contacted following the hint from the Sheffield group, '... we will not concede to each other when we have a good thing before us ... Mr Paine was so good as to offer to draw up something for us if he had a little more time.'

Another week went by, and it seems Mr Paine did not find the time. However, Margarot now produced a draft which was accepted with only a few amendments. The preamble to the agreed Address declared, 'Man as an Individual is entitled to Liberty – it is his birthright'. Each member of society 'voluntarily yielded up only as much [of his rights] as was necessary for the common Good. He still preserved a Right of sharing in the Government of the Country – without it no Man can with Truth call himself Free'. But now that right was withheld from the majority and the few who still held it abused it. So several Societies about the country had been formed to correct 'this Evil'. Among them 'the Corresponding Society which with modesty intrudes Itself and Opinions on the Attention of the Public in the following Resolutions ...'

Eight resolutions were listed. They asserted that every individual had the right to vote (only 'Non-age, Privation of Reason or Offence against the Rules of Society can incapacitate him'); that every citizen had a duty to keep a watchful eye on the Government; that because of the partial representation there were 'oppressive Taxes, unjust Laws, restrictions of Liberty and wasting of Public Money'; that the only remedy was 'a fair, equal and impartial Representation of the People'; and finally the Society expressed 'their Abhorrence of Tumult and Violence', and stated that 'as they aim at Reform, not Anarchy, Reason, Firmness, and Unanimity are the only Arms they themselves will employ, or persuade their Fellow-Citizens to exert, against the Abuse of Power'.

The only question that remained was, who should sign the Address? (Or as Hardy put it, 'Who should put the bell about the cat's neck?') One after another the committee members demurred, fearing the loss of their employment or earnings. Eventually, it fell to Hardy who agreed he had the least to lose, though he thought that being 'so obscure an individual his name could add no consequence to it'. In fact, this agonising was unnecessary, for Horne Tooke took it upon himself to send the manuscript to the printers, having signed it in Hardy's name!

One thousand copies of this Address were printed in the form of hand-bills which were distributed in the streets of London and, according to Hardy, 'throughout the country'. Copies were sent to the Societies for Constitutional Information in London, Sheffield and Manchester. It was also published in some newspapers.

Within seven weeks came a Proclamation from the King directed against 'divers wicked and seditious writings'. The primary target was Paine's *The Rights of Man*, but no doubt the LCS Address had been seen by government ministers, and they may well have regarded it as an example of the unrest that they thought was being stirred up by Paine's book.

20

1792 was not a happy year for John Cartwright.

But we need to backtrack a little. In 1788 he had bought a large estate near Boston in Lincolnshire at that time a centre of woad-growing. He soon perceived that rivalries among local farmers were lowering market prices and inflating wages and he persuaded them to form a small cartel to maintain a good price and low wages. It was not an action which would have endeared him to the working-men of the LCS if they had heard about it. Nor would they have been sympathetic to Cartwright's reaction to the violent protests by farm-labourers a couple of years later when their living was threatened by an influx of cheap Irish labour at harvest-time. He urged the other farmers to arm themselves. 'One musket and one bayonet in defence of peace and law,' he wrote, 'is a match for a score of scythes in the hands of men conscious of criminality.'

All this was far from life on the streets of London, where the news was dominated by dispatches from Paris. Cartwright initially welcomed the reports he read in the papers. In fact he was moved to write to the President of the Committee of Constitution of the States General congratulating the French people who 'are not only asserting their own right, but they are also advancing the general liberties of mankind'. But it was not a sentiment he retained as the revolution developed.

For the most part, however, his preoccupation with his new estate kept him away from political activity at this crucial time, though he did attend the dinner to celebrate the second anniversary of the falling of the Bastille. This gave the Duke of Newcastle the excuse to deny him promotion in 1792 to the vacancy of Lieutenant-Colonel in the Nottinghamshire militia and to appoint another officer in his place as Major. It was a dreadful blow to Cartwright. He challenged the legality of the Duke's action and only after a year of protest did he accept his dismissal, then publishing a 'letter' to the Duke (112 pages plus a 45-page postcript!) declaring among other things that 'your conduct has been illiberal, dishonourable and unconstitutional'.

Poor John! Robbed of his most cherished honour, his only official standing. But at least he could, and did, retain the title of major. He was undoubtedly right in accusing the Duke of Newcastle of political discrimination for the establishment generally was becoming extremely nervous about the growing unrest in the country. This they attributed, with some reason, to the rapid spread of Paine's provocative polemics which seemed to threaten revolutionary infection from across the Channel. But the Duke's fire was misdirected for Cartwright, despite the cap of liberty he had put on the regiment's buttons, clearly repudiated Paine's republicanism. On April 11th 1792 he met with 'a group of gentlemen', mostly members of parliament, for the purpose of heading off the dangerous revolutionaries. They called themselves 'Friends of the People' and stated their cautious objectives as:

> First – To restore the freedom of election, and a more equal representation of the people in Parliament.

> Secondly – to secure to the people a more frequent exercise of their right of electing their representatives.

These vague and gentlemanly aims were endorsed by about a hundred signatures – John Cartwright Esq (not Major!) among them. The intention was that 'all friends of Parliamentary Reform [would] form themselves into similar Societies, on similar principles, in all parts of the kingdom' (though necessarily of more humble membership). The committee of twelve gentlemen, of whom eight were members of parliament, drew up a somewhat fuller statement for approval at the following week's meeting; in this the Society committed itself to introducing a reform bill into the next session of Parliament.

It is hard to be sure what Cartwright thought he was doing in this company. Was it sheer naivety on his part? Or was he convinced that he should ally himself to all reformers, however tepid? Other members of the SCI, which was now becoming more forthright and demanding, were not of this opinion. They had never thought it likely that parliament would spontaneously reform itself, and they responded with a scornful letter to this new society which 'announces itself to the world as Friends of the People'. Reform would only come about when there was an irresistible demand for it in the country and 'without the fellowship of the people your association will surely crumble to dust'.

It happened that Cartwright was in the chair at the SCI meeting which approved this letter and it therefore carried his signature. Apparently he saw no anomaly in signing this dismissive reaction to the declaration which he, as one of the Friends, had also signed. Others did, and five of the MPs forthwith resigned from the newly formed society when this came to light. Those who stayed agreed to send a short letter to the SCI refusing 'all further intercourse'.

Cartwright returned to his cultivation of woad.

21

By the King

PROCLAMATION

George R

Whereas divers wicked and seditious writings have been printed, published and industriously dispersed tending to excite tumult and disorder, by endeavouring to raise groundless jealousies and discontents in the minds of our faithful and loving subjects respecting the laws and happy constitution of Government, civil and religious, established in this kingdom; and attempting to vilify and bring into contempt the wise and wholesome provisions made at the time of the glorious Revolution, and since strengthened and confirmed by subsequent laws for the preservation and security of the right and liberties of our faithful and loving subjects: And whereas divers writings have also been printed, published and industriously dispersed ... And whereas we have also reason to believe that correspondences have been entered into with sundry persons in foreign parts with a view to forward the criminal and wicked purposes above mentioned: And whereas the wealth, happiness and prosperity of this kingdom do, under Divine Providence, chiefly depend on a due submission to the laws, a just confidence in the integrity and wisdom of Parliament ... And whereas there is nothing which we so earnestly desire as to secure the public peace and prosperity and to preserve to all our loving subjects the full enjoyment of their rights and liberties, both religious and civil: We therefore being resolved, as far as in us lies, to repress the wicked and seditious practices aforesaid and to deter all persons from following so pernicious an example, have thought fit, by the advice of our Privy Council, to issue this our Royal Proclamation, solemnly warning our loving subjects. . . to guard against all such attempts which aim at the subversion of all regular Government within this kingdom ... and earnestly exhorting them at all times, and to the utmost of their power, to avoid and discourage all proceedings tending to produce riots and tumults: And we do strictly charge and command all our Magistrates in and throughout our kingdom of Great Britain that they do make diligent enquiry in order to discover the authors and printers of such wicked and seditious writings as aforesaid, and all others who shall disperse the same: And we do further charge and command all our Sherrifs, Justices of the Peace, chief Magistrates in our cities, boroughs and corporations and all other of our Officers and Magistrates throughout our kingdom of Great Britain, that they do in their several and respective stations take the most immediate and effectual care to suppress and prevent all riots, tumults and other disorders ... And we do further require and command all and every of our Magistrates aforesaid, that they do, from time to time, transmit to one of our Principal Secretaries of State due and full information of such persons as shall be found offending as aforesaid, or in any degree, aiding or abetting therein: It being our determination for the preservation of the peace and happiness of our faithful and loving subjects, to carry the laws vigorously into execution against such offenders as aforesaid.

Given at our Court at the Queen's House the 21st day of May 1792 in the thirty-second year of our reign

GOD SAVE THE KING

This document might be thought to betray a certain governmental anxiety, not to say 'a panic dread of change', as Wordsworth put it. When it was debated in the House of Commons it was not without its critics. Charles Grey affected to see it as directed towards his recently founded Society, Friends of the People; but the Government would hardly have wheeled out the big guns to attack so innocuous a group. He suggested that 'if there were writings which ought to have been prosecuted ... then His Majesty's Ministers ought to have prosecuted them'. Apart from such seditious publications, 'there ought to be full liberty of publication of political opinions'. Instead the House was called upon to support 'a Proclamation inciting Magistrates and others to turn informers and to exert themselves in a way destructive of all good neighbourhood and society by placing men as spies over each other'; and Grey moved an amendment censuring the Government for these failures.

Several members spoke in support of this amendment and they, as well as the Tory speakers on the other side, were more explicit about the real villain whom the proclamation sought to suppress – Thomas Paine. So when the minister, Mr Dundas, set out to defend the government, he found it necessary to explain their tardiness in taking action against the libellous sedition – this much everyone seemed to agree upon – of Mr Paine. At first they considered this 'so bold, so profligate, so far beyond the bounds of reason' that they could ignore it.[6] Only later with the publication of Part II of *The Rights of Man*, did they take alarm.

In fact, on 14 May a summons had been issued against Paine's printer, J. S. Jordan, and a week later, on the very day of the Proclamation, Dundas had filed an 'information' against Paine himself requiring him to appear before the King's Bench on 8 June. Apparently undaunted, Paine published an open letter to Dundas in which he affirmed his authorship of the book and his continuing adherence to its contents. The SCI, which had already circulated 6000 copies of its denunciation of the Proclamation, now passed a resolution in support of Paine and printed 12000 copies of his Open Letter. Many members of the Society, including Cartwright and Horne Tooke, opposed these actions, being keen to distance themselves from this republican firebrand. But they were over-ridden by the more militant members who in the last months had pushed the Society into a much more strident stance. They were now supporting and encouraging the working-men's clubs and societies which were mushrooming all over the country during 1792: the SCI sent copies of their resolutions to groups in Sheffield, Norwich, Southwark, Derby, Belper, Birmingham, Aldgate, Manchester, Liverpool, Cambridge and Glasgow, as well, of course, to the LCS.

The Court of the King's Bench duly heard the information against

Paine on 8 June, decided that this 'wicked, malicious, seditious and ill-disposed person', as the government indictment put it, had a case to answer. A date in December was set for the hearing. In August it happened that Paine was awarded French citizenship by the National Convention and was then invited to represent the Pas de Calais at the Convention. In view of this, and with the threat of arrest rumoured to be imminent, he decided to repair to France. The story has it that the warrant for his arrest arrived at Dover twenty minutes after his boat had set sail, though others say that the government let him go, being only too glad to see the back of him.

22

Grey's prediction that the King's Proclamation would 'incite magistrates and others to turn informers ... placing men as spies over each other' was fulfilled all too soon. On 7 June the LCS committee recorded that 'certain magistrates who thinking every measure legal in consequence of the King's Proclamation and, in their hurry, stumbling over the Brothels, the Gaming Houses and the receptacles of public depredation fostered under their wing, dared to threaten harmless Publicans with putting a stop to their licences, if they admitted to their houses any sober, industrious body of Tradesmen, presuming to discuss political subjects. Thus ... several Divisions found themselves at a loss for houses to meet at.' The following week they recorded that 'the Committee itself assembled for the last time at the Bell in Exeter Street' – the proprietor, Robert Boyd, having been among those so threatened. After this they were obliged to meet in their own private houses, or like the displaced Divisions, in auction rooms and other places not subject to licences.

This was a severe inconvenience to the Society and probably involved it in additional expense. But there was another, more sinister, development of which the committee was unaware. On 7 October the Minister Lord Grenville received a letter from one signing himself 'Mercator' and claiming to be a member of the London Corresponding Society. He described meetings that he had attended at which 'the sacred character of His Majesty is held up to Public ridicule, His Ministers are constantly calumniated, and every principle on which they act misrepresented'. The writer asserted that 'Mr Paine, Horne Tooke, his nephew Mr Vaughan lend no small assistance towards exciting the People to rebellion', and went on to offer further information if 'your Lordship will be pleased to signify in the most guarded manner in the Daily Advertiser'.

No more is heard of this 'Mercator' unless he became one of the government spies whose reports appear amongst the LCS papers in the Public Record Office. The first of these is from one George Lynam and is dated 29 October 1792. His first few attempts to infiltrate meetings were unsuccessful but he persevered and was soon accepted into Division 12; within a month he actually got himself elected as delegate to the General Committee. From this central vantage point his reports flowed for the next eighteen months, unsuspected by the members until June 1793 when Willian Baxter lodged an accusation against him. Though, even then when they heard the evidence, the committee decided in favour of Lynam and he continued to report.

A second spy began reporting on 14 November 1792. This was George Munro, an army captain. He was perhaps a more educated man than Lynam, who was an ironmonger, although his spelling was equally wayward. He evidently did not find the LCS members very congenial company: 'the whole of them except the Delegate [to the committee] appeared to me to be the very lowest tradesmen, they were all smoaking pipes and drinking porter' – though he conceded that they were 'extremely civil'. The delegate he refers to was 'a young man who had a large bundle of papers before him that he would not oppen till I was gone and would not admit me as a Member without being proposed and recommended by two of the Members'. That was in the 15th Division. He tried again in the 13th, where 'they were more decent but also extremely low. The house and the people in it impress'd me with much horror as the people below stairs seemingly consisted of nothing but Thieves and pickpockets'. As a stranger he still found himself regarded with suspicion until he tried the 5th Division where 'the Deligate's Name was Thompson, discovering that I was a Countryman of his (for he was Scotch) I was admitted with little difficulty'. He reported that 'the Scociety's intentions seem that of corrupting the minds of the lower order of people by inflaming their imaginations with imaginary grievances working them up to comit some great excess which may alarm and throw the Country with the greatest Confusion.'

It seems that once admitted as a member in one division, Munro had no difficulty in attending the meetings in others. (He reported in

November 1792 that there were 22 or 23 divisions in all.) He went to divisions 10, 6, 3 (attended, he said, by more than 200 pople, and where 'I met a Mr Hardy who seem'd the leading man'. Again he notes that 'all the Divisions are attended by the very lowest tradesmen, and the most of them seem Scotch shoemakers'.(!)

Later in November yet another spy began reporting. This was Christopher Kennedy, a carpenter and a Bow Street constable. He submitted reports on the constitution of all the Divisions 1 – 16, giving their meeting places and in most cases the names of their delegates. He appears to have had no difficulty in gaining admittance except at Division 8 where he was 'very ill treated and was informed that no man in office [presumably including that of constable] was suffer'd to enter the room'. He withdrew 'and as I was going I rec'd a Kick in the Side on the Stairs'.

Although the members were generally unaware, though sometimes suspicious, of this infiltration, they could hardly have failed to notice attempts by police and others to disturb their meetings. In a draft history of the Society, Hardy wrote that the committee 'did not meet two nights in one place for several weeks ... but shifted their place of meeting every week to avoid the interruption of police officers who were prowling about seeking whom they might devour – we knew that they could not legally interrupt us but by their clamour and threats they might prevent us from quietly meeting together and impede us in doing the business of the Society'.

This sort of treatment grew in intensity following the formation of 'The Association for Preserving Liberty and Property Against Republicans and Levellers' initiated by John Reeves, a talented lawyer with some government service. It was founded at a meeting at the Crown & Anchor Tavern on 20 November 1792 with the intention of organising a network of societies whose object would be 'to support the Laws, to suppress seditious Publications and to defend our Persons and Property against the innovations and depredations that seem to be threatened by those who maintain mischievous opinions founded upon plausible but false reasoning'. There is some evidence to suggest that the Association was formed with government connivance and possibly helped with government money. Certainly its committee was packed with establishment figures, distinguished barristers, MPs, and members of the aristocracy. But the ears and eyes of the Association – people who sent in information eavesdropped in tavern or barber-shop and forwarded to the Government – were ordinary people disturbed by the alarmist rumours propagated in the press and by various 'anti-Jacobin' bodies of which Reeves's Association was the most active. Their reports were used as the basis for prosecutions of which there were many up and down the country, most of them resulting in prison sentences and fines.

The LCS was understandably worried by this new threat. The committee saw it with some reason as being directed mainly at their Society and they drew up a placatory explanation of the LCS objectives for insertion in a Sunday newspaper ('if it could be got in') and for '500 large copies to be stuck up in the streets'. Their statement began with a refutation of the suggestion that they were 'levellers'. In fact the seventeenth-century Levellers would have sat quite comfortably in the eighteenth-century Corresponding Society (see Chapter 23), but what was at stake was what had come to be attributed to them which was a misinterpretation of their belief in 'equality' and in particular their supposed desire to redistribute property so that everyone would be on the same 'level'. That this was an erroneous belief was irrelevant: what mattered was that this was what was conveyed by the label. To dissociate themselves from it, they wrote: 'We know that the Wages of every Man are his Right; that Differences of Strength, Talents and Industry do and ought to afford proportional Distinctions of Property which when acquired and confirmed by the Laws, is sacred and inviolable'. They went on to explain their objective of parliamentary reform: 'If at the Revolution [of 1688], this Country was adequately represented, it is so no longer and therefore calls aloud for REFORM'. They would watch 'with Patience and Firmness' the ensuing sessions of parliament 'from whom we have so much to hope and little to fear ... It may prove the Source of our Deliverance. Should it not, we trust that we shall not prove unworthy of our Forefathers, WHOSE EXERTIONS IN THE CAUSE OF MANKIND SO WELL DESERVE OUR IMITATION.'

Following this the committee approved a letter, drafted and signed by Margarot, to the Home Secretary Henry Dundas, giving the reasons for their Association and calling on the Government to protect them in the pursuit of their constitutional rights, even demanding that he (Margarot) should be put on trial should their campaign for reform be deemed illegal.

It is not recorded whether Mr Dundas ever replied to this letter. Probably not. However, it was not Margarot who was arrested – at least not at this juncture – but a poor illiterate bill-sticker, William Carter, whom the LCS had engaged to post up their Address about the streets. He was apprehended in the act by a Bow-street runner and was subsequently sentenced to six months in jail. The committee were appalled by this: they opened a subscription for the support of Carter's family, and they severely reprimanded the printer, Grant, who had engaged Carter but had failed to instruct him to stick the bill at night when he might not have been apprehended.

23

In the latter half of the eighteenth century political debate took place within terms of reference very different from today's– and there was a different set of terms of abuse. Foremost among these was the label 'Jacobin' (an eighteenth-century equivalent of such modern dirty words as 'communist', 'terrorist', 'hippy' or 'leftie'); any eighteenth-century reformer was likely to encounter such a slur. This chapter takes a brief look at the history of this bogey-word, together with some of the others that were current in the political vocabulary of the period.

The term Jacobin was taken from the French revolutionary grouping of this name, which had originated in a quite innocent debating club that used to meet in the convent of Jacobins in Paris in the 1780s. As the popular clamour grew, this club expanded and spawned other meetings both in the metropolis and in the provinces. They called themselves Jacobin clubs. They had a broader membership than their parent society, attracting a significant number of artisans. After 1789 the Jacobins became an identifiable party, more radical than other revolutionary groupings. It was here that the dreaded Robespierre found a home – dreaded, that is, on this side of the channel. The Jacobins, under Robespierre's leadership, seized power in 1793 and, egged on by the even more militant sans-culottes, they became identified with the awesome Reign of Terror.

The popular societies in Britain gave rise, precisely because they were popular – of the people – to frantic fears of a copycat rising in this country. The societies became stigmatised, with lurid tales of murderous mobs baying for blood. Once they had been dubbed Jacobins, when the country went to war with France the term gathered the added imputation of treachery – fifth columnists as we would call them now. So we find Pitt the Younger, when he was introducing his gagging measures in the Commons in 1799, speaking of 'the pestilential breath of Jacobinism'. And the Whig spokesman, Mr Tierney, confessed he was 'fearful of being called a Jacobin' simply because he opposed the government. 'Either a man must be a Jacobin,' he said, 'or give proofs of the most obsequious loyalty.' Burke estimated that there were some 80,000 Jacobins in the country: 'pure Jacobins, utterly incapable of amendment; objects of eternal vigilance'.

This was the language of the relatively benign proceedings of Parliament. Outside, it could be more dire. When Hardy was brought to trial, a witness related how, 'even in the dead of night, they have come where I have lodged and insulted us ... and have sworn they would pull down the house and burn it, calling us Jacobins, and calling the house Jacobin-hall, because the Society used to meet there.'

Another example of a bogey-word was the term 'leveller' which implied, among other things, someone who would reduce everyone to the same level and in so doing would rob people of their private property. The term leveller was originally coined by men who were rebelling against enclosures in Leicestershire and Warwickshire in 1607 – levelling the newly planted hedges and newly erected fences. It came into more general use forty years later when it was applied to a fundamentalist religious sect that flourished during the English civil war and formed a part of Cromwell's army. This group was not concerned with hedges, more with social inequalities. They tried to head off the parliamentarians from reneging, as they saw it, on the radical purposes that had been the mainspring of battle. They fought for individual rights, for religious tolerance, for equality under the law, for equal participation in parliamentary elections – for much the same things, in fact, as were being championed by the radical reformers of the eighteenth century. But by then the Levellers had come to be associated in the popular mind with support for such things as equality of incomes, or equality of ownership. So when Reeves founded his 'Association for Preserving Liberty and Property Against Republicans and Levellers', the LCS, believing correctly that this Association was directed against themselves, felt it important to publish a refutation of any suggestion that they could be tarred with the Leveller brush; though interestingly, in view of the charges later to be brought against them, the suggestion that they were republicans did not seem to worry them so much.

In 1794 Wordsworth, tongue in cheek, wrote: 'I am of that odious class of men called democrats'. To our ears it is strange to find this as a term of abuse, but democracy used to be thought of as a revolutionary menace. For example, the Duke of Richmond, himself a radical reformer, wrote in his *Letter to Col Sharman,* 'I am not for a democratic, any more than for an aristocratic or monarchic government, solely; I am for that admirable mixture of the three.' A democrat was seen as one who, following the French example, would destroy the established power of the aristocracy and of the monarchy; a reform of parliament that included universal suffrage was thus seen as subverting the very constitution, tantamount to treason. However the modern attitude to democracy was beginning to creep in, and many reformers would claim the term unashamedly. Thus Thelwall, commenting in 1795 on the unintentional effects of Burke's *Reflections on the Revolution in France,* claimed that the book 'has made more democrats, among the thinking part of mankind, than all the works ever written in answer to it'. But this position remained unusual; generally people were anxious about the term. For instance, at one point the radical societies in Norwich wrote to Hardy seeking assurance that the LCS still abided by the Duke of Richmond's reform plan, and enquiring whether 'it is the secret design to rip up the monarchy by the roots, and place democracy in its stead'. Monarchy and democracy at that time were considered incompatible.

24

Until the impact of Reeves' association began to be felt, the LCS appears to have been inconvenienced but not intimidated by the actions of magistrates, police and others that followed in the wake of the King's Proclamation. The Society steadily expanded, reaching perhaps six hundred members by the end of 1792. Correspondence with other societies continued; and the committee saw to it that the public were regularly informed of their existence and of their case for reform. A second Address was published only a few days after the King's threatening proclamation; it described the Society's aims, constitution and ways of working, and included a fairly detailed appendix on the current state of parliamentary representation. A third Address appeared in mid-August which re-iterated the LCS proposals for reform and enumerated the expected changes that would follow a reform of parliament. These were largely culled from Paine's *The*

Rights of Man, Part II which had been published earlier in the year:

> Soon then should we see our Liberties restored, the Press free, the Laws simplified, Judges unbiassed, Juries independent, Needless Places and Pensions retrenched, Immoderate salaries reduced, Taxes diminished and the Necessaries of life more within the reach of the poor, Youth better educated, Prisons less crowded, old Age better provided for, and sumptuous Feasts, at the expense of the starving poor, less frequent ...

Two thousand copies of this Address were printed and numbers were sent to the SCIs of London, Manchester and Sheffield, to the Borough branch of the Friends of the People (with whom the LCS was in regular contact), to Edinburgh and to the *Patriot* (a fortnightly paper published in Sheffield).

In September the committee accepted the offer of five hundred copies of an Address which had been received by a group called the Constitutional Whigs from the Jacobin Club at Cherbourg. This stimulated them to consider sending an Address to the people of France and Margarot was deputed to prepare a draft. He also initiated the first attempt by the LCS to organise a concerted action by asking the various reform societies that were proliferating across the country to sign the Address. In the event only four of the societies agreed to this request, though the committee evidently thought this was enough to justify their claim that it came from five thousand British Citizens.

The Address assured Frenchmen, that though 'foreign robbers are ravaging your territories ... [a reference to the invading armies of Austria and Prussia that had been relentlessly advancing on Paris in the summer of 1792, with the aim of restoring the authority of Louis XVI, who at that time was still nominally occupying the throne] ... there are Britons, 5000 of them at least, who manfully step forth to rescue their country ...':

> Be assured, Frenchmen, that our number increases daily ... Men ask each other, What is freedom? What are our rights? Frenchmen, you are already free and Britons are preparing to become so ... Dear friends, you combat for the advantage of the human race. How well purchased will be, though at the expense of much blood, the glorious, the unprecedented privilege of saying Mankind is free! Tyrants and tyranny are no more! Peace reigns on earth! And this is the work of Frenchmen!

On 1 November 1792 the French Ambassador, M Chauvelin, received the LCS deputation – Hardy, Margarot, Martin and Walne – and Margarot read out their Address. Chauvelin undertook to convey the document to the Convention where, according to Hardy, 'it was received with rapturous applause ... The National Convention distributed copies to all the Departments of France where it caused a very great sensation.' By this time the French had finally abolished their monarchy and had declared a republic. Louis was guillotined on 21 January 1793 – 'the foulest and most atrocious act the world has ever seen', according to Pitt. On 1 February France declared war in Great Britain.

Now the LCS became even more suspect. Their expressions of sympathy with the enemy were not merely seditious, but traitorous. With the Association set up by Reeves becoming more and more aggressive – aided and abetted by the press, and from the pulpit – the Society, still but a year old, found itself embattled. Recalling these days several years later, Hardy wrote: 'All that hubbub and noise throughout the country disorganized the London Corresponding Society very much – Many of the Members were also alarmed and fled to different parts of the country – some went to America – others who were great declaimers in the society slunk into holes and corners and were never heard of more – others of the violent orators deserted and joined the Standard of the enemy. The comparatively few who remained firm and true to their first principles and determined to persevere – were obliged to hire private houses and Auction rooms at great expense – the members were obliged to double their weekly pay and double their diligence.' Perhaps Hardy was guilty of some embittered exaggeration in his recollection of these events for the minutes of the committee do not suggest any great diminution of activity. For instance in January 1793 they instructed Secretary Hardy to open correspondence with Bath, Glasgow, Durham, Banff and Dundee. Evidently, societies were continuing to mushroom across the country, significantly in Scotland. And if there were some members 'slinking into holes and corners', the Society was still gaining new recruits. It is true, however, that the committee rejected the idea of a publication justifying the execution of the French king – on the grounds that 'our Enemies might infer ... that we wished a similar Event taking place in this country'.

One among the new recruits was John Thelwall who was to become a prominent member, and one of the 'great declaimers of the Society'. He had had only an elementary schooling but had read widely. After a few years working in the family shop, and then as an apprentice to a tailor, he became clerk to an attorney. He left this post in his early twenties, to devote himself to his real interest, in literature. He wrote poetry and was an active member of a debating society (later becoming friendly with Coleridge and Wordsworth). In 1790 he assisted with Horne Tooke's first, and unsuccessful, campaign for a seat in parliament. Horne Tooke subsequently helped him in his literary aspirations and probably gave him some financial assistance. Thelwall's own political ideas developed through his debating at the 'spouting shops', and he came to the LCS via his membership of the Southwark branch of the Friends of the People – an organisation he probably found too tame for his radical taste. Even in the LCS he had to be restrained upon occasion. By the time Coleridge and Wordsworth welcomed him into their Somerset retreat, Thelwall had acquired a notoriety that caused these poets to hold him in some awe. 'A man of extraordinary talent,' said Wordsworth. 'Intrepid, eloquent and honest,' thought Coleridge.

Another important recruit was Felix Vaughan who was a nephew of Horne Tooke. He was a barrister and came to the LCS first as a visitor from the SCI. The spy Lynam noted his presence on 29 November 1792 when he offered a draft of an address which became the Society's first response to Reeves's threatening society. Lynam notes that 'Mr Vaughan most strongly recommended good order and peaceable conduct'; and with his legal background this observation points to Vaughan's useful role in keeping the Society on the right side of the law. Thelwall and Vaughan were both, in their different ways, to play vital parts in the future life of the Society.

25

In December 1792 delegates from as many as seventy Scottish societies met in Edinburgh in what they called a 'Convention' – a term with a respected history, but which at that time carried ominous overtones because of its association with the French revolutionary National Convention, which had usurped the functions of the Legislative Assembly. The Edinburgh gathering, however, was by no means revolutionary: it was far too disparate for that, the delegates representing societies of gentlemen as well as of tradesmen and artisans. Though originally formed on the basis of interests ranging from the slave trade to the cost of living, from the Test Acts to the corn laws, these societies were united to the extent that they believed parliamentary reform would ameliorate their several discontents. The tone of their discussions was generally moderate, though it was occasionally disturbed by such fiery interventions as that from one Thomas Muir, who brandished an Address from the militant United Irishmen that struck the more faint-hearted as 'possibly treasonable'.

The Convention adjourned, charging its Secretary, William Skirving, to contact the English reform societies, and taking an oath (borrowed from the French) 'to live free or die', and resolving to reconvene in April 1793. The Scottish authorities were alarmed. Within a month of the adjournment, Muir was arrested, released on bail and re-arrested the following July to be tried for sedition at the end of August.His trial, and those of others which were to follow, seem to belong more to an Alice-through-the-looking-glass concept of justice than to serious legal procedures. [7]

Muir, himself a qualified member of the Scottish Faculty of Advocates, chose to defend himself. The judge was Lord Justice Braxfield, a tyrannical character who used to boast 'Bring me the prisoners and I'll find you law' – and if he couldn't find it he would make it up, it seems. In Muir's trial this was not too difficult for, unlike the English charge of 'seditious libel', the offence of sedition in Scotland was so ill-defined (rather like today's 'disturbing the peace', though more serious) that Braxfield felt himself free to tailor it to fit the case. He ignored Muir's learned defence and bullied his hand-picked jury into returning a guilty verdict. He then astonished them by sentencing the hapless prisoner, not to a month or two in jail as they had expected, but to transportation for 14 years!

Closely following this so-called trial came that of Reverend Thomas Fysshe Palmer, an Eton and Cambridge graduate, now a preacher at Montrose. He was charged with having 'put into the hands of George Mealmaker a writing of seditious import', and with having 'wickedly circulated ... a number of the said seditious and inflammatory writing', including 100 copies to William Skirving. The offending document contained such incitements as:

> The time is now come, when you must either gather round the fabric of Liberty to support it, or, to your eternal infamy, let it fall to the ground ... You are plunged into a war by a wicked Ministry and a compliant Parliament ...

the end and design of which is almost too horrid to relate – the destruction
of *a whole people merely because they will be free.*

In the course of the trial George Mealmaker admitted that he was
himself the author of these fighting words. Nevertheless Palmer was
held to have been 'accessory to correcting it' and of having got it
printed and circulated. He was duly found guilty. The trial started at
8.30 in the morning: by 2pm he had been sentenced to 'banishment
forth of Great Britain for seven years with certification of death in case
of being found returning from banishment within that period.'[8]

Protests at the conduct and outcome of these trials reverberated all
the way down to London: Muir and Palmer were seen as martyrs.
Their ill-treatment was debated in the House of Commons on a motion
put by Charles Grey, which was, of course, defeated. But if the object
of the savage sentences was to stifle the Edinburgh Convention, it
succeeded only in scaring off the 'gentlemanly sector' leaving the floor
to the more vociferous intellectuals and the angrier tradesmen. They
resolved to meet on 29 October 1793. Skirving rather belatedly sent
letters, as instructed, to the LCS and SCI in early October. The LCS
committee, after referring the matter to the Divisions, decided to send
two delegates to be chosen at a General Meeting. In the meantime they
appointed a special committee to draw up instructions to the delegates.
These stipulated that they should not depart from the original objects
of the Society, viz to obtain by 'lawful and rational' means annual
parliaments and universal suffrage. There were then enumerated half-
a-dozen subsidiary objectives, and the instructions ended with the
admonishment that 'delegates were to be punctual and frequent in
corresponding with the Society'.

The General Meeting was held on 24 October at 'Citizen Briellat's'.
Briellat was a pump-maker in Hackney Road who had a field which he
offered for the Society's use. It was the first time that they had
attempted an open-air meeting and Hardy records that 'the announcement in the Newspapers caused a considerable stir'. A large crowd
began to pack the streets in the vicinity. Passers-by inquired what all
the excitement was about and 'many curious and laughable observations were made, some saying "Tom Paine was come to plant the tree
of liberty" and others that "the French Jacobins were come" and others
that "the London Corresponding Society were met to lower the prices
of provisions"'.

Members of the committee conferred with the local magistrates who had gathered in the nearby Nag's Head. It was estimated that between two and four hundred LCS members were present together with perhaps 4000 spectators. It was not an easy setting in which to conduct the business but they did succeed in their main aim – to elect two delegates for the Edinburgh convention: it was decided to send Margarot and Joseph Gerrald.

At this point the magistrates sent a message asking for the business to be expedited 'on account of the increasing Concourse of the Populace'. Votes of thanks were quickly made to the magistrates, to the High Constable and to 'our Fellow Citizens, the Spectators' and the meeting was closed at 3.30. It had been a difficult afternoon, but at least it had given the LCS welcome publicity. Hardy concluded 'Many who came there to ridicule and abuse went away converted and afterward joined the Society and became zealous promoters of the Cause'.

The committee felt well pleased but for one sour event at the end: when most of the throng had dispersed Briellat was arrested and charged with using 'seditious language'. At his trial it turned out that the offending remarks had been made not at this meeting (in which Briellat had taken no active part) but at a tavern twenty months previously. He was sentenced to a year's imprisonment with a £100 fine. By English (if not Scottish) standards this seemed vindictive and it is hardly surprising that Briellat, when he was released from jail, felt he had had enough of his home country and decided to emigrate to America.

26

Margarot and Gerrald set off for Edinburgh on 30 October, the committee having agreed to pay their fares and expenses to the tune of nine shillings for each day they stayed at the Convention. They were joined on the coach by George Sinclair who had been appointed as the SCI delegate. They had a long, uncomfortable journey ahead of them.

In fact the Convention had opened the day before they left London, and the 160 delegates, mostly from societies in the south of Scotland, were already busily debating various motions, while soldiers patrolled the streets outside and Muir and Palmer idled in jail, awaiting their transportation to the other side of the globe. After four days the delegates dispersed. The London delegates at that time were trundling through the turnpikes in Lincolnshire. They did not get to Edinburgh till 6 November.

However, the Convention had appointed a committee, which was still there to welcome the three dusty travellers, as well as a delegate from Sheffield, Matthew Browne, and two from Ireland. Margarot immediately took charge, firing the debate-weary committee with new life. He was not one to understate his case. There were 50,000 reformers in Sheffield alone, he declared; there were 30 flourishing societies in Norwich which had deputed him to act for them: a convention held in England next year would represent up to 700,000 men. Parliament would not be able to ignore them. Buoyed up by his rhetoric, the committee re-convened their Convention, and 180 delegates met once more on 19 November.

They now found themselves in a much more electrifying atmosphere thanks to the dynamism of the English delegates. Margarot took the chair and now roused the delegates as he had inspired their committee. Gerrald mocked the way they called each other 'Gentlemen', and thenceforward 'Citizen' became the correct mode of address. He also persuaded the citizens that they were about the Lord's business by introducing prayers for the Almighty's blessing at the opening and closing of each session. As the fervour rose they talked about moving the Convention to England. York was favoured. Then came the most daring idea – that a secret committee should be appointed poised to re-convene the Convention when and if events moved to a crisis; specifically, if foreign troops landed (mercenaries from the German states were rumoured), or if there was a suspension of the Habeas Corpus act, or if the Government tried to outlaw a convention.

This was heady stuff, creating a feeling of conspiratorial action. But at seven o'clock the following evening the sheriff's men burst into the room that Margarot and Gerrald shared, arrested them both and siezed their papers. Sinclair and Skirving were also taken into custody, although the latter was very quickly released. The next day the Lord Provost appeared in the hall with a posse of constables and ordered the chairman to dissolve the meeting. This being refused a curious charade ensued. The Provost said he would have to remove the chairman by force but then appeared reluctant to do so. Eventually it was agreed that he could use 'token force' which would not be opposed, and he eased the chairman from his seat. The gathering dispersed – and straightway reassembled in another hall.

By the next day, all the prisoners (except, of course, poor Palmer and

Muir) had been released on bail. Margarot took the chair at the new meeting-place, and was dramatically recounting the story of his arrest when the Lord Provost put in a second appearance. A similar charade was enacted but this time the delegates had nowhere to reassemble. In any case the Provost now issued a proclamation forbidding all assemblies within his jurisdiction. The Convention had run its course.

News of these events took some time to reach London. The delegates wrote to their committee each week and Hardy sent a regular twelve guineas each fortnight, though the committee were finding it difficult to sustain this flow of money. There were collections and Thelwall donated the proceeds from a series of twice-weekly political lectures that he started for this purpose; and being a passionate and entertaining speaker he drew large audiences. The Norwich societies were also sending some money to Margarot.

When news came of the delegates' arrests, it was greeted with consternation by their friends in London. With the fate of Muir and Palmer still fresh in their minds they had been aware of the risks that Margarot and Gerrald were running. But now the worst had happened and they were powerless to help. Letters from Edinburgh became more frequent and more desperate. Then came news that Gerrald was on his way back to London – remarkably, he had obtained permission from the Court 'to settle some family matters' and had had his trial postponed to 27 January. But to Hardy he wrote that he was coming 'in order that a public and spirited attack should be made upon Dundas to give an account of the infamous and unconstitutional proceedings which have, of late, taken place at Edinburgh'. A letter from Margarot suggested that their trials would actually result in effecting a reform 'or at least work up the minds of the people to that pitch necessary for effectuating it'. He responded impatiently to a request for an account of their expenditures: 'Upon my word fellow citizens we have already more upon our hands than we can well manage without wasting time [on this].' Two days later he wrote again asking for further protests to be made with 'perhaps a Procession of Members of the Society'. And on 30 December he wrote asking Hardy to arrange subpoenas to be served on Pitt, Dundas and the Duke of Richmond.

These letters sound an understandable note of desperation, mixed with a certain failure to keep in touch with the reality of the situation. Margarot was isolated; Gerrald had escaped, leaving him, it seemed, to his fate. What were his distant friends doing to help him? Why were they fussing about money when should they be stirring up protests at his treatment? Who was there to help him? But he was convinced that his innocence would become self-evident, and decided to conduct his own defence. He constructed fantasies of calling government ministers into the witness-box, of a popular uprising as his arguments were heard. He had come a long way in the twenty months from the days when he was reluctant even to put his signature to an LCS Address. Now he faced alone – though he was unable to look squarely at the reality – the merciless force of Scottish justice, a system in which, as the editor of the *Edinburgh Gazette* wrote to Hardy, 'indictment has become synonymous with conviction'.

The trials began in early January. The first to be brought before Lord Braxfield and four other judges was Skirving. The charge was sedition, so vague a term, protested Skirving, as to be meaningless. But he was assured by one of the judges that 'it is well understood by everyone'. Skirving was also defending himself, but his two-hour speech to the jury did nothing to prevent a savage sentence of fourteen years transportation.

Margarot faced his judges the following week. He tried, but of course failed, to expel the Lord Justice-Clerk from the Bench as being too prejudiced to give him a fair trial. And indeed Braxfield's summing up reads more like a speech for the prosecution:

> The crime of sedition consists in poisoning the minds of the lieges ... Now gentlemen, take a view of the conduct of this meeting ... It is at a time when we are at war with a great nation, a cruel ferocious nation ... I say, bringing it forward at that period is strong proof that they were enemies to [the constitution]. I appeal to you all, that you are living under a happy government in peace and plenty, in perfect security of your lives and property, the happiest nation upon the face of the earth ... For a set of men in that situation to raise a faction in the minds of the lower order of the people, to create disaffection to the government ... I say these things appear to be ... sedition of a very high order.

After such words from the 'ablest of judges', how could a jury find the prisoner innocent? Margarot was sentenced to fourteen years transportation.

Charles Sinclair, as an SCI delegate, was of course representing a group of gentlemen rather than a rabble of the lower order. He was moreover defended by Henry Erskine. After a number of adjournments his case was abandoned. There was a plausible rumour that he gained his liberty by undertaking to act as informer for the government.

There remained Joseph Gerrald. He did not appear on the date fixed for his trial and it was assumed that he had skipped bail. Indeed there were friends in London who had urged him to do so, notably his much respected former schoolmaster Dr Parr. Gerrald may well have intended not to put his head in this noose, but many of his colleagues in the LCS thought otherwise. A resolution was tabled '... If he should avoid his Trial in Edinburgh [it] would materially injure the Cause of Liberty, tend directly to encourage future Prosecutions & set an example of timidity ...' His friend Godwin also urged him to return: 'Your trial ... may be a day such as England and I believe the World, never saw. It may be the means of converting thousands, and progressively, millions, to the cause of reason and public justice.' Gerrard succumbed to these stern urgings and set off to meet his judges. Perhaps his Maker saw things differently – his coach was caught in a snowstorm. But it only delayed his arrival and his trial was postponed until March. He soon found the court's vindictiveness had not abated. Like the others, he was found guilty, and was given the same sentence – though in his state of health (he was consumptive) he would not be expected to survive much more than a year of the hardships to which he was being condemned, let alone fourteen years. It was a death sentence.

The Scottish Martyrs, as they came to be called, were kept in the Tolbooth and later taken to the hulks moored in the Thames to await the next convoy to the antipodes. Here they were visited by their friends and given what small comfort was possible. In April Margarot, Skirving, Muir and Palmer were transferred to the transport ship *Surprize* moored at Spithead. In a letter to Mr Dundas (a copy of which was printed in the *Morning Post* on 10 April, Margarot explained that he had written to the captain of the ship about his wife's passage and having had only the vaguest reply he asked the Minister for the Home Department to give instructions that she should be treated with the 'utmost, delicacy, attention and respect'. It appears he received no such assurance for Mrs Margarot did not travel to Australia. Perhaps Dundas was riled by Margarot's concluding paragraph:

> I cannot close my Letter without returning to you my unfeigned thanks for all the severities I have experienced by your express order. Bolts, padlocks, handcuffs, confinement in damp pestilential places, along with common felons and a stinted ship allowance similar to theirs – all these, Sir, though highly preju-

dicial to my three fellow sufferers, and likely to prove fatal to two of them, have had a very different effect upon me – they have convinced me that, however you think proper to punish my body, my mind preserves its independence and remains invariably attached to the cause of the People, and to a thorough Parliamentary Reform, which you but accelerate by such repeated severities.

Hardy visited the Martyrs at Spithead for the last time. He reported that, contrary to Margarot's account, the prisoners were 'exceedingly merry', except for Muir who was 'very dull and pensive'. They were being well treated by the captain who seemed a 'very good kind man and bears an excellent character'. This was a curiously sanguine view of his friends' fate. Hardy must by now have realised that the enterprise he had committed himself to was faced with a merciless opposition. To argue that he was merely joining a campaign for reform would, a year earlier, have been a reasonable position. But this was no longer tenable: the weapons of oppression were to be relentlessly used against him. He was not faced with 'good kind men', but with a fierce aristocracy determined to suppress any attempt to claim a voice for the lower orders. That these first victims were actually men of the middle order was a stern signal to others that the ignorant plebeians were not to be supported in their insubordination.

27

The making of a martyr usually involves a violent death followed by an express passage to heaven. The Scottish Martyrs, though, suffered only virtual death sentences, supplemented by a few years in hell.

In the earlier part of the eighteenth century transportation had meant removal to the American colonies, but the war there put an end to this. The criminals – mainly condemned for thefts of paltry quantities of food, etc – were housed for a time in the dreadful 'hulks'; these were old warships or troop transports, with their masts and rigging removed, which were moored in the Thames or at Portsmouth, slowly to rot. The convicts too might rot, crammed into these stinking sinks, with 14-pound irons fastened to their legs to discourage thoughts of a desperate leap to freedom by water. They were taken ashore in chain-gangs to work at cleaning the filthy river shores, incidentally providing the locals with an alternative entertainment to watching the lunatics in bedlam. But much as the public enjoyed this, the threat of epidemics of typhus and cholera incubating in the hulks was a strong motive for keeping convicts away from the vicinity of so many unconvicted souls.

Captain Cook's voyage of discovery in 1770 opened up the possibility of Australia (or New South Wales, as Cook called it) as an alternative dustbin into which to tip these unfortunates, and in 1787 the first convoy of transports set out on its eight-month voyage, through storms and doldrums, to Botany Bay. It was a gruelling passage for the men and women cooped up below decks. In 1793 Sir Charles Bunbury drew the attention of his fellow members of Parliament to this inhumane process.

> Of the 500 passengers [sic] on board the *Neptune*, but forty-two were able [on arrival] to crawl over the ship's side; the rest were carried, and eight out of ten died at Sidney Cove. The details of the sufferings of these wretched convicts would be tedious and painful ... they were equal to any endured in the slave ships. In another instance, out of 1863 on board the *Queen* and other transports in 1791, 576 on landing were sent to hospital.' [9]

Palmer, Muir, Skirving and Margarot were among those in the transport *Surprize* which sailed out of Portsmouth in February 1794. This ship had earlier been one of the second fleet to make the voyage and the scandalous loss of life then may have been reason enough for conditions to be slightly less intolerable on this voyage. At any rate there were fewer than ninety convicts in place of the usual two hundred odd. But this was only a relative relief: they were still condemned to hours and days and months in the ill-ventilated semi-darkness below decks, assailed by the stench from the bilges, tossed on their wooden boards in the storms, stifled in the airless heat of the tropics, frozen as the ship approached the Antarctic, plagued by rats and mice.

Such privations may well have contributed to the decline in Margarot's mental state, which had already verged on the irrational in Edinburgh. He now turned against his friends, taking the unlikely story to the ship's captain that his three fellow martyrs were plotting mutiny. He was always articulate and it seems the captain was convinced – or perhaps it was simply that he could not risk ignoring the tale. The result was that Skirving, Muir and Palmer spent the rest of the voyage on short rations in the additional discomfort of the punishment cage.

Not surprisingly, once disembarked at Sydney his former friends would have nothing to do with their accuser. 'Margarot is expelled,' Muir wrote to a friend at home. Thus isolated, Margarot continued his new-found career as spy/informer, now directing his attention to army officers, reporting on their supposed corruptions to the civilian authorities. He endured seventeen years of this twilight life before buying a passage back home. Here he plunged into the murky regions of ultraradical politics, all the time watched by government spies. One of his plots, reported by the informer Arthur Kidder, involved as a fellow conspirator Arthur Thistlewood, who was later hanged for his part in the Cato Street conspiracy (This was, reportedly, a planned insurrection to be started with the assassination of as many government ministers as could be managed.) Margarot and Thistlewood's scheme was no less desperate – they planned to go to France and make contact with Napoleon, to urge him to invade England without further delay, in order to establish a republic there. Of course the plan failed, another of Margarot's unrealised fantasies. He died in poverty only five years after leaving the antipodes.

Having survived the rigours of the convict ship, life for Palmer and Muir must have seemed relatively benign. Food was short as it was for the whole community but they were spared the bondage of most convicts, the chain-gangs, the forced labour, the brutal whippings. They had been banished to this benighted settlement more to get them out of the way than as a punishment and in fact Palmer was told that he would be given 'every indulgence' as long as he refrained from any political activity. They were given a few acres of land to work, and they also made a bit of money trading in rum – a tolerable life but hardly satisfying intellectually. After three years Muir was driven to attempt a daring escape, rowing out to an American ship as it prepared to sail. He subsequently transferred to a Spanish vessel but unfortunately by this time war had broken out between Spain and Britain, and after many harrowing vicissitudes, including the loss of his left eye, he landed in a prison in Cadiz. This lamentable story ended more happily, however: he was recognised by the French as an English republican and was restored to friends in Paris, where he subsequently lived for a few years. At first he was something of a celebrity, but after a while he subsided into poverty, until in 1799 he died.

Of the others, Palmer was joined in Australia by an old friend, John Boston, who had voluntarily emigrated with his wife in order to keep Palmer company. Together they embarked on several enterprises:

making beer, making soap and finally going into ship-building. After his seven-year sentence was finished, Palmer bought and restored an old Spanish warship, in which he hopefully set sail for England. But the ship was not equal to an ocean voyage and he had to abandon it at a Spanish outpost near Guam where, like Muir, he was imprisoned. He died there of cholera in 1802.

Skirving was given 100 acres to farm. His friend Gerrald, who had been transported a year after the others, was already ill when he left England and he arrived in Sydney too weak to undertake any physical work. He was given a cottage near the harbour and died a few months later, in March 1796. Skirving died only three days later.[10]

28

John Cartwright's withdrawal to his woad-growing lasted throughout 1793, and only occasionally was his voice heard from this blue haven. He was moved, for instance, to publish his thoughts on the occasion of the decapitation of the King of France. Although he had incited the farmers of Lincolnshire to confront protesting labourers with muskets, he now explained that he doubted the competency of human authority to punish with death: and in the case of guillotining the King he could excuse it even less than usual.

An extract from a December 1795 issue of the *Sun* indicates the nature of the 'usual' hangings of eighteenth century Britain:

> The following capital convicts received sentence of death, viz. *Mary Ashe* and *Jane Hutton* for robbing Henry Seymour of a silver watch – *Ann Tracey*, *Peter Tracey*, a boy, and *Mary Browne*, for robbing William Witnel of a hat and Holland apron – *Mary Thorpe*, a girl of 14, for robbing her master – *William Owens*, for burglary, and *Lockey Hill* for horse-stealing.

In such a context one might suppose that the execution in Paris would cause no great sensation, but regicide was a thing apart. It was inexcusable. It was, as Cartwright wrote: 'in the highest degree impolitic', likely to do 'great disservice to the cause of freedom'. From such dispassionate reasoning, Cartwright then quickly subsided into a vehement denunciation of 'the mean, revengeful, murderous spirit of a small faction, the demagogues of an ignorant rabble ... a faction who are a disgrace to humankind'. He contrasted these 'enemies to justice, to humanity and virtue' with the magnanimity of a considerable number whose votes were for saving the King's life. Ironically that number had included Tom Paine, whom Cartwright regarded as a disreputable rabble-rouser, a dangerous republican rather than a virtuous humanitarian. As a Deputy in the French Convention, Paine had urged that the king and his family be sent to America.

Cartwright's censorious words may sound not very far from Burke's sneer at the 'swinish multitude', or to Pitt's description of the king's execution as 'the foulest and most atrocious act the world has ever seen'. But he did proceed to warn against 'permitting our own rulers' to use 'this act of wickedness' as a pretext for 'involving us in a war against the French people ...'. However, within less than a month of this publication England was at war with France.

Towards the end of 1793, Cartwright learned of the savage sentences which Palmer and Muir had suffered at the hands of the Scottish judiciary. A letter from Muir, written from one of the hulks in the Thames, was published in the *Cambridge Chronicle*. On reading this, Cartwright was moved to write to his old ally the Duke of Richmond. 'Read that letter, my Lord, I beseech you; and read also the trial of the writer. If he merit the treatment he received, I, also, and your Grace, ought to be cast into the dungeons amomg felons. But if he be the virtuous victim of that corrupt and arbitrary system which your Grace and I have laboured to reform – it is needless to say more.'

But more *was* needed, and was not said: not by the Duke, and not by Cartwright.

29

The Edinburgh convention alarmed the government. They were faced with widespread protests at the savagery of the sentences, but when a motion was introduced in the Commons asking that a reform of certain aspects of the Scottish criminal law should be considered, the Home Secretary responded aggressively. He said that, in view of 'the numberless seditious writings daily circulated ... by a large body called the London Corresponding Society', the present laws of England were inadequate and that they should consider introducing those aspects of Scottish law here. (This was the first time that a government minister had named the LCS as one of its prime targets.) It was as though, like a drug addict, they were driven by their own failings into yet more ill-conceived extremes. They had thought to quell the worrying ferment with the King's May proclamation, and with the subsequent proceedings against Paine, around whom they had thought the trouble centred. But although they had seen him off (to France), and had stimulated the magistrates and police into repressive harryings, as well as having received the added help of Reeves' aggressive cohorts of informers, to their consternation the agitators continued to gather support.

The press tried to laugh off the Scottish Convention: 'A few obscure people in Edinburgh have met in what they call a Convention ... They may be allowed to amuse themselves in this way, but to print their proceedings in the news-papers is rather too much on the brogue' (*Cambridge Chronicle*, 7 December 1793). But for the government the very word 'convention' implied a threat to supplant the established order with a gathering of demagogues feeding, and fed by, a bloody mob ranging the streets outside: the word sent shivers up the governmental spine. It had happened in France, it could happen in Britain too. The hundred or so delegates from the fringes, with their secret committees and inflated oratory, were readily transformed four hundred miles away into an image of imminent insurrection.

These fears were bolstered by the reports of the spies who knew how to interest their nervous paymasters. One of them, Gosling, said that his governmental contact (an under-secretary of State, William Wickham) had 'desired me if I should hear any further conversations about Arms to direct my attention particularly to disciver whether they ... really intend to procure Arms or had any secreted'. So in the early months of 1794 came a flutter of reports to feed the ministerial nightmares:

... there was a general Conversation about an insurrection here and Gerrald say'd in Scotland they wod soon break out. (Spy Lynam, 20 Jan)

Armed Associations are I perceive now set on foot by the Rich – wherefore should the Poor do the same ... (Margarot in letter to LCS Committee, 24 Jan)

Jones added that Orders were given in this Country for many thousand Daggers – & he pulled out his Rule to shew me the Size wch was nine inches

– that the intention of them was to be carried under the Coat, and that it was determined to put an end to Mr Pitt & all the leading Men on that side.' (Spy Groves, 13 Feb)

... some very violent Persons present who gave toasts & sung songs of a very treasonable tendency – One person drank a Speedy Guillotine to the King.' (Spy Taylor, 1 March)

Among other conversations on this Evening, Wright said he thought it would be an advisable measure for the Society to learn the use of a Musket and how to form themslves into Ranks, and that he meant to move in the Committee of Delegates that each Delegate be directed to recommend such Measure to his respective Division.' (Spy Metcalfe, 2 April)

Nodder ... went to the house of the Bookseller Spence who is the depot for the Holborn division [of the LCS]. In an upstairs room, behind closed curtains, they exercised with mop-handles, under the direction of a gunsmith ... Nodder also reports on the existence of a military society organised by a few of the most desperate of LCS: they were to be supplied with guns by Williams, a gun-engraver, and to be drilled by Orr, a Camberwell tailor. They met in places which were also used by the LCS. (Summary of report by the spy Nodder, 7 April)

Pearce and two or three others pulled out large Knives with white Ivory or Bone handles and long blades (pointed) ... and said almost all Citizens had them. I enquired of Pearce where I could get One – he reply'd Green sold them ... They are what the french call Couteau Secret – you cannot shut them without being acquainted with the Secret Spring. (Spy Groves, 14th April)

Some members of the LCS undoubtedly did feel that they should be prepared to use arms. Most notable among these were John Franklow, a tailor who in 1793 had been appointed as assistant secretary, and Thomas Spence, a one-time schoolmaster in the north of England who had moved to London and opened a bookstall, 'The Hive of Liberty'. Spence published a long-running periodical *Pigs Meat* (echoing Burke's 'swinish multitude'), and a constant stream of cheap pamphlets. He came closer to qualifying as a 'Leveller' than any other LCS member, and doggedly argued for the confiscation and redistribution of private estates. None of this, of course, endeared him to the authorities, and he was several times arrested, being charged with anything from sedition (selling Paine's *The Rights of Man*, for instance) to high treason.

Franklow is credited with having founded the organisation known as the Lambeth Loyal Association (LLA) – the word 'Loyal' being appropriated from the language of Reeves and the Church & King faction. In one sense it was a splinter group of the LCS – only LCS members were accepted into the LLA – but it was never recognised as such by the LCS leadership. Spence was Franklow's enthusiastic lieutenant, if not the real organiser of the LLA. He made his premises available for its meetings at which members would be drilled in the use of broomsticks (in the absence of actual pikes) and guns. A colourful uniform was devised – the spy Nodder describes Franklow appearing in 'blue coat & red collr, buff on white waisct and breeches, black Stiff Stock & a military Cock'd Hat with a large Cockade' – but it is doubtful whether any but he and Spence were ever thus decorated. In fact it is not at all clear just how many members the LLA attracted – probably very few. The spies never reported seeing more than eight men at the drilling sessions. But the very existence of such a group was enough to disturb the Privy Council when reports reached them.

To add to these alarms the government began to get reports that the LCS was planning another Convention, this one to be held not in the distant fringes of the kingdom but somewhere in England itself, and possibly involving all the numerous reform societies from up and down the country. Ministers did not have to rely on their spies for this information: the two general meetings which the LCS called to decide upon their plans were publicly advertised and reported in the press, though of course the spies filed their own lurid reports.

The first of these meetings was held at the Globe tavern on 20 January 1794. The spy Taylor estimated that one thousand people attended, an exaggeration perhaps, but certainly there were so many as to cause the floor to collapse and the meeting had to adjourn to another room. Once safely re-settled, the gathering heard an account of Margarot's trial. This provoked great consternation, and was an effective curtain-raiser to the main business of the afternoon: to approve an 'Address to the People of Great Britain and Ireland' and to consider a number of resolutions related to it.

John Martin, who chaired the meeting, had written the Address, although Thelwall later asserted that Horne Tooke had had a major hand in its preparation. It opened by deploring the loss of life, the damage to commerce and the increase in taxes occasioned by the war with France. It proceeded to denounce the encroachments on civil liberties stemming from the war by 'this corrupt and unrepresentative government', drawing particular attention to the trials and inhumane sentences in Scotland. 'We must now chuse at once either liberty or slavery for ourselves and our posterity...' The Address concluded: 'THERE IS NOT A REDRESS FOR A NATION CIRCUM-STANCED AS WE ARE, BUT IN A FAIR FREE AND FULL REPRESENTATION OF THE PEOPLE'.

Following the adoption of the Address, a resolution was passed which instructed the Committee to meet daily while Parliament was sitting so as to be ready to call a 'General Convention of the People' if and when any of the following measures was introduced:

– to allow the landing of foreign troops in Great Britain or Ireland
– to suspend the Habeas Corpus Act
– to proclaim martial law
– to prevent people meeting in Societies for Constitutional Reform
– other measures of a similar nature.

In fact, only a week after this, the first of these conditions was fulfilled: the King ordered a corps of Hessian troops who had been kicking their heels on board ships anchored off the Isle of Wight, to disembark, some on the Isle, some at Portsmouth. There were objections registered in parliament. Charles Grey, maintaining that foreign troops could not legally land in Britain without the prior consent of parliament, put forward a motion condemning the action. It was defeated by 184 votes to 35. Lord Stanhope spoke on similar lines in the Lords, even suggesting that people finding these troops in their midst should 'forcibly seize and arrest, as the Law directs, the Traitor who should be guilty of such High Treason against them'.

No such traitors were apprehended, despite the LCS distributing 50,000 copies of Stanhope's speech. Nor was a Convention convened as it should have been according to the General Meeting's resolution. The Committee seemed to falter. They appointed a sub-committee – Martin Baxter, John Williams, Thelwall and Moore – 'to consider Measures to be pursued during the present posture of Affairs & to be a secret one.' Given its covert nature, the activities of this committee are obscure but it was probably responsible for a letter which was circulated to other Societies in March. If their action was hesitant, their words were urgent:

CITIZENS! The critical moment is arrived, and Britons must either assert with zeal and firmness their claims to Liberty or yield without resistance to the chains that ministerial usurpation is forging for us. Will you co-operate with us? ...

The letter went on to explain the need to act before a Convention Bill was adopted by Parliament to outlaw any gathering 'of the different Societies throughout the Nation'.

Hessians and Austrians are already among us: and, if we tamely submit, a cloud of these armed Barbarians may shortly be upon us. Let us form then another British Convention. We have a central situation in our view ... but which we forbear to mention (entreating your confidence in this particular) till we have the answer of the Societies with which we are in correspondence.

This letter was signed, 'in Civic affection', by T. Hardy.

The secret committee then wrote to the SCI seeking their support in calling a General Convention, and the SCI responded positively by suggesting a meeting between five delegates from each of the two Societies. One of the LCS men, Moore, took the chair at this meeting – 'a tall Man, the most gentlemanly of the Delegates', according to William Sharpe, one of the SCI's delegates. (Evidently, the SCI men, for all their professed sympathy, were still uncomfortable relating to the 'tradesmen and mechanicks' of the LCS.) Apart from agreeing to a further meeting, little was accomplished, largely because of an apparent filibuster led by one of the SCI delegates, Thomas Holcroft, who introduced a 'Conversation on the Powers of the Human Mind', which lasted an hour-and-a-half.[11]

However, their next meeting, on 9 April, was more to the point: much of it was absorbed in a discussion of the title 'convention', which probably carried too many challenging associations for the more cautious SCI delegates. As events turned out this could be seen as a wise caution, but Thelwall insisted that it would be cowardly to avoid this title for a meeting whose purpose was, after all, to convene the people to press for a fair parliamentary representation. Eventually they reached a compromise recording that:

It appears to this Company very desireable that a Convention or General Meeting of the Friends of Liberty should be called, for the purpose of taking into consideration the proper methods of obtaining a full and fair representation of the People.'

They also recommended that a joint Committee of Correspondence & Cooperation be set up. This would 'hold personal communication' with members of other societies as and when such people should be in London. (Subsequently Horne Tooke became a member of this committee. along with Joyce, Lovett, Bonney and Wassel from the SCI.) Thus the once sedate Society that Cartwright had founded committed itself to militant action. What its founder would have thought can only be guessed. He was still in distant Lincolnshire.

The second General Meeting was convened a few days later, at half-past three in the afternoon, on 14 April. It was held at an inn at Chalk Farm where, to the landlord's consternation, some 2000 people crammed into his gardens. The magistrates installed themselves in an upper room, instructing the landlord to serve ale to none but themselves, thus depriving their unfortunate host of the considerable sales he might have anticipated on this unusually warm afternoon.

John Lovett, the chairman, began by warning the company of the presence of spies and informers who might attempt to provoke 'riot and disorder'. The crowd groaned when John Richter told them that the Friends of the People had refused an invitation to attend, then cheered when they learnt that the Society for Constitutional Information had accepted. Thelwall intervened to ask the spies to be sure to tell Harry Dundas of the SCI's involvement: 'He and Billy Pitt must shake at the information of such a number of respectable citizens joining in so glorious a cause'. He went on to mock the infiltrators, but told the crowd not to 'hurt a hair of the poor creatures' heads ... our proceedings will make their Masters' hairs stand on end'.

At one point the landlord's wife appeared at an upper window, crying out in some distress for the meeting to disperse and go to some other place: the magistrates were threatening to withdraw her husband's licence. But where could two thousand people re-assemble? Lovett told her that to disperse now would cause great tumult and they would rather continue their business where they were in a quiet and peaceable manner.

And so they did. They approved a series of ten resolutions. These expressed indignation at the 'late rapid advances of despotism'; detestation of the 'flagrant and flagitious proceeding of the Court of Judiciary in Scotland'; and approval of the Convention in Edinburgh and the conduct of their delegates there; they asserted that any attempts to violate the remaining laws in England 'would be regarded as dissolving the social compact between the English Nation and their

Governors'; and expostulated about the 'outrageous attempts to intimidate the free spirit of Britons by subjugating them to an army of mercenary cut-throats'; they suggested that Ministers advising the King to arm one part of the people against the other should recall that such a measure brought Charles I to the block and drove James II from his throne, and that they should therefore consider whether they were not guilty of High Treason; and finally they affirmed their belief that 'the friends of freedom could not fail of crowning with ultimate triumph the virtuous cause in which we are engaged'.

The business of the afternoon was concluded by approving an Address to Joseph Gerrald, still languishing in one of the hulks at Portsmouth: 'our beloved and respected friend and fellow Citizen, a Martyr to the Glorious Cause of Equal Representation ... for us you are suffering transportation to New Holland where your sufferings may be alleviated by remembrance of your virtuous Conduct and by the Esteem of your fellow Citizens ... We will continue to demand our rights ... We shall never forget your Name, your Virtues, nor your great example. – [Signed] John Lovett, Chairman, & Thomas Hardy, Secretary.'

These resolutions marked the Chalk Farm meeting as the point at which both Societies turned from mere persuasion to provocative demands. And the government was duly provoked.

NOTES

1. While staying with the Hardys, Equiano was perhaps finishing the extraordinary story of his life which was published under the title *The Interesting Narrative*. It is currently published by Penguin Classics.
2. Quoted in Claire Tomalin, *The Life and Death of Mary Wollstonecraft*, p.141
3. Olivia Smith, *The Politics of Language*, pp36 ff.
4. The population was then only about 10 million, so this sale is equivalent to about 1 million copies today; and this takes no account of the much lower literacy rate that then obtained – at most two out of every three adults could read at all and far fewer would have been fluent enough for sustained reading.
5. In fact Burke's book provoked 50 or more pamphlets and tracts, though none but Paine's had any significant impact.
6. Quotes from *The Times*, 28 May1792.

7. The legal aspects of these trials are well expounded in Alan Wharam, *The Treason Trials*, 1794.

8. Quotes from *The Times*, 19 September 1793.

9. Reported in the *Annual Register, 1793*.

10. Much of the information in this chapter is taken from *The Fatal Shore* by Robert Hughes.

11. Thomas Holcroft, a well-known playwright of this time, was a close friend of William Godwin. Hazlitt wrote of his membership of the SCI: 'he did not approve of many of their proceedings ... but still he conceived that this was not a sufficient ground to absent himself from their meetings, as such an over-scrupulousness would exclude all those who were best calculated to prevent such societies, in their too great ardour to do good, from doing ill ... [He] sometimes spoke but was oftener silent.' Not on this occasion, apparently.

PART III TRIALS

30

MONDAY 12 MAY 1794

With the sun barely above the horizon, a party of six men strode in wordless intent along Piccadilly. At their head was John King, private secretary to the Rt. Hon. Henry Dundas, and John Gurnel, one of the King's Messengers; following were Edward Lauzan, the son of another King's Messenger, two Bow Street constables and, some way behind, an older man, a locksmith, less purposeful in his tread.

The group stopped outside No 9, the leaders conferring in hushed tones. All was quiet within. Mr and Mrs Hardy still lay asleep in their bed in the ground-floor parlour (the upstairs rooms were let out to lodgers and the Hardys lived in this one room alongside the 'shop' which was where Thomas worked and dealt with customers). Mr King nodded to young Lauzan who stepped up to the door and hammered upon it with his fist. The two constables positioned themselves behind him. Two or three passers-by, arrested by the sudden noise that disturbed the early morning quiet, stopped on the other side of the street to see what this should mean.

Inside the house Hardy, now awakened, rose from his bed, threw on a few clothes and went to see what the commotion was about. Opening the door, he was thrust backwards by the inward rush of men. One of the constables seized him. Lauzun shouted, 'Mr Hardy, we are here to arrest you!' 'Arrest me? On what charge? Where is your authority?' Lauzun waved a paper in his face. 'For treason, sir. We are arresting you for High Treason. Here – here is the signature of the Minister, Mr Dundas. We are authorized to search your house.' He stabbed the document with his finger, and hastily returned it to his pocket.

Hardy was bundled into the parlour, where his wife sat in bed white-faced and trembling, realising that what she had long feared was now actually happening. Immediately, the intruders began their search, pulling papers and books from the shelves. Finding the bureau locked, they demanded the keys. Hardy refused. Lauzun seized a poker to force open the drawers. At this Mrs Hardy protested. The bureau, which she polished weekly, was the only piece of solid oak furniture in the house. Mr King stayed Lauzun's clumsy assault and sent instead for the locksmith waiting outside who quickly opened the drawers with his skeleton keys and then set about opening the two trunks from which the plunderers scattered yet more papers. Mr King, scanning the documents, was still not satisfied and the invading party removed themselves and their prisoner into the shop where Hardy, disdainfully silent, watched their fruitless scrabbling among his tools and shelves; as he later recorded, 'they expected no doubt to find treason hatching among the boots and shoes'. And they might have found, if not treason, at least what Mr King particularly wanted, if they had noticed the large drawer beneath the cutting-board. Left alone at last, Mrs Hardy hurriedly dressed herself, though she was unable to tidy her hair before the invaders returned and, to her consternation, proceeded to strip the bed to search under the mattress.

Outside, two hackney carriages had drawn up in front of no.9. The group opposite, now grown to half-a-dozen, waited and watched. Eventually they saw Hardy being led from his house by Mr Gurnel, followed by one of the constables carrying in each hand two bundles of documents tied into large silk handkerchiefs. They watched the three men get into one of the carriages and saw their friend driven away. Shortly afterwards Mr King and Mr Lauzun re-appeared with the other constable carrying a cornsack filled with books and pamphlets which they heaved into the second carriage. The sad-faced locksmith shuffled off down the street.

When all the searchers had gone, two of the watchers crossed the street and Mrs Hardy let them into the house. They heard her tearful account of what had passed: she had been afraid of this, she had heard that American Colonel Smith say, 'Hardy, the Government will hang you'. They'll hang him, won't they? The two friends gave what reassurance they could, leaving her with a cup of tea and the promise to 'send the wife round to help clear up this mess'. Before they left however they went into Hardy's shop and found the drawer beneath the cutting-board untouched and the Journal of the Society still lying there. They took it off to some safer place.

They had barely gone when Mr King returned, having met by chance the spy Taylor who told him exactly where Hardy kept the Journal that they had failed to find. As Mrs Hardy opened the door he pushed her aside and rushed into the shop. The drawer was unlocked, but empty.

In the meantime, Hardy was being driven to Mr Gurnel's house where he was to stay for the next fortnight or so and where, he recalled later, he was 'treated very civilly'. The Gurnel family gave him breakfast and settled him in an upstairs room, but he had barely time to ponder his situation before another carriage came to carry him off to Whitehall where he was faced with the first of a series of interrogations by members of the Privy Council, including Pitt, Dundas, various noble lords and, to Hardy's chagrin, John Reeves, whose notorious Association for the Preservation of Liberty and Property had been harrying the LCS over the previous six months. Pitt was particularly restless at these inquiries. Unable to keep his seat, he paced the room, pausing every so often to stare out of the window, then bounding across to Dundas to shout 'What does he say? What does he say?' By contrast, Hardy maintained his customary imperturbability, acknowledging his handwriting on some of the documents placed before him, denying knowledge of others, briefly answering the insistent questions.

In the afternoon of this same day the House of Commons received a short Address from the King:

> His Majesty having received information that the seditious practices which have been for some time carried on by certain societies in London, in correspondence with societies in different parts of the country, have lately been pursued with increased activity and boldness, and have been avowedly directed to the object of assembling a pretended general convention of the people, in contempt and defiance of the authority of parliament, and on principles subversive of the existing laws and constitution, and directly tending to the introduction of that system of anarchy and confusion which has fatally prevailed in France, has ordered that the books and papers of these societies be seized and laid before the House of Commons to take measures to prevent further prosecution of these dangerous designs.

That evening Mrs Hardy, alone in her ravaged home, imagined her husband in some dungeon, or already hanged for all she knew, just as Colonel Smith had prophesied. Small groups of LCS men gathered in their houses and in taverns to talk over the events of this agonising day.

News spread that not only Hardy but Daniel Adams, secretary of the SCI, had been arrested. Rumour had it that he too had been charged with treason. The two secretaries. There were those who urged some violent action; some wanted the convention to be immediately called; others thought that they should lie low. The committee members decided to meet the following evening.

31

The House of Commons met on Tuesday, the day after Hardy's arrest, to consider the King's message. A so-called Committee of Secrecy was appointed, to examine the papers that had been seized at the time of the arrests and report back to the House.

Several Divisions of the LCS met that evening and the General Committee gathered in nearly full strength in Thelwall's house. They formed themselves into a 'Committee of Emergency', with the intention of inviting to it one in every ten members from the Divisions. Thelwall explained the law of treason (the word Mrs Hardy had heard bandied about by the men who had arrested her husband) and they persuaded themselves that there was not the slightest ground for charging Hardy with such a crime. The committee resolved to support their imprisoned secretary 'to the utmost of our ability'; and they further resolved to 'conjure [the Divisions] not to be discouraged or alarmed at the violent proceedings of the Government, but to pursue, with unabated ardour, the objects of their Institution'.

The committee dispersed to communicate these brave words to the Divisions. Thelwall saw them go and then himself prepared to leave to deliver one of his lectures. But as he stepped into the street he was seized by a posse of Bow Street runners, headed by Constable Walsh, a man whom Thelwall had taunted as a spy at the Chalk Farm meeting. Some of the committee saw this happening, followed the coach into which Thelwall had been bundled and saw him taken to the Secretary of State's Office. Here he was interrogated by the Committee of Secrecy but, unlike Hardy, he refused to answer their questions, so that the only information they gained was that his name ended in two 'l's, rather than one.

This was the third arrest. Others followed with menacing profusion in the next few days: Joyce and Martin were arrested the next day, 14

May, and on the 16th Lovett, Richter, Bonney and Horne Tooke were gathered in. The latter pair were SCI members as was the Reverend Jeremiah Joyce, who was arrested at Lord Stanhope's house where he was employed to tutor Stanhope's two sons. In fact Tooke had helped to trap both himself and Joyce with one of his mischievous pranks. When he realised that one of the frequent visitors to his house was a government spy, he had begun to feed the man with titillating inventions, culminating in a hint that he was master-minding plans for an imminent insurrection. When the government intercepted a letter to him from Joyce containing the phrase 'Is it possible to get ready by Thursday?', they pitched in with what they thought were pre-emptive arrests of the two supposed plotters.

Bonney, an attorney, was still more unfortunate in his arrest. According to a report in *The Times* of 17 May:

> He had been in the afternoon to *Gurnell*, the Messenger's house, and said he had come as Counsel to Citizen Hardy, and was employed by a society of gentlemen [the SCI, presumably] who were determined to protect him. He demanded a copy of the warrant under which Hardy was arrested, which being refused, he behaved in a rather riotous manner. The Privy Council, who were then sitting, on being told what had passed, ordered Bonney to be taken into custody, which was accordingly done.

On the day of Tooke's arrest, Pitt presented the first report of the Committee of Secrecy to the House of Commons. The Committee had concluded, he declared, 'that a plan had been digested and acted upon ... the object of which was nothing less than to assemble a pretended Convention of the People ... a general representation of the Nation superseding [Parliament and Government]'.[1] Elaborating upon this in a lengthy speech, Pitt again and again dangled the French bogey before the assembled Members. The SCI, for instance, were 'communicating with individuals of that country at the moment when France was about to engage in war with this country'. And they had tried to disseminate the French doctrines 'thro' every part of their own country, through all the population and manufacturing towns ... and to excite groundless jealousies, to raise discontents, and to mislead the understanding of every class of Society'. Not only that, but the SCI had supported the British Convention held at Edinburgh, 'a Convention that avowed the principles of universal suffrage and annual Parliaments and what they were pleased to call the unalienable right to reform'.

As for the LCS, it was 'the most despicable and contemptible in the opinion of many in point of education and talents'. Pitt declared that it was easy to see the inseparable connection of the LCS with 'that line of plunder, with that spirit of robbery, which has assumed the name of liberty in another country', going on to add that 'Although in one view it might be considered as contemptible, yet in some views of the subject they were important and formidable'. He drew attention to the fast growth of the Society, and 'a rapid increase among the lower orders propagating their baneful doctrines through every dark and obscure corner of the Kingdom'. The 'baneful doctrines' were of course the support for universal suffrage and annual Parliaments and in Pitt's view such participation of the 'lower orders' would inevitably lead to anarchy, as had happened in France.

He went on to make a brief reference to the Committee's belief 'that it was part of the plan to put arms into the hands of those whose minds the Society had endeavoured to corrupt', though he admitted that this required further inquiry. Now Pitt had reached his main purpose. He asked the House to approve the suspension of the Habeas Corpus Act – 'the Constitution itself being in danger then suspension ought to be acquiesced in by every man who loved the Constitution'.

In reply, Fox was dismissive of Pitt's alarms. He was sarcastic about the Committee's 'revelations'. Most of the documents it had examined, he said, had been with them for years, and had been published in the daily papers. The inferences that had been drawn were quite unfair. As to the fact that the Societies had planned to call a Convention, 'it by no means followed that it was for the purpose of assuming the functions of Parliament'. There was nothing wrong with Conventions – many Members had attended Conventions, as he himself had done. Nonetheless, the House voted on the second reading, by 186 votes to 29, to suspend the Habeas Corpus Act – 'this great guardian of personal liberty,' as Fox put it – and the Bill then went before the House of Lords.

Introducing the Bill into the Lords, Lord Grenville painted a lurid picture of the schemes of this 'set of desperadoes': 'All supremacy was to be destroyed – all property was to be aggregately divided and ... THE PRESENT ROYAL FAMILY WAS TO BE MURDERED'. The conspirators planned to 'overturn all the present laws of the land, and to place in the chair some modern Robespierre, who should deluge the land not only with Royal blood but with that of every person who was loyal to the Sovereign and attached to the Constitution of his country'.

With such a prospect before them it is small wonder that only seven of the 102 noble Lords present voted against the suspension.

The government could now proceed with their arrests without the necessity of laying charges. By the end of the month another eight men had been locked away in the Tower of London. Hardy too was transferred there on 29 May, to the sound of a cannonade from the guns of the Tower. This was not to greet him as he at first thought, but in celebration of the 134th anniversary of the restoration of the monarchy; which occasion, Hardy comments in his *Memoir*, 'ought now to be blotted out as a day of rejoycing'.

Four of the captives now in the Tower had been members of the SCI; the other thirteen were from the LCS. There was also a Mr Saint, a publican and Secretary to the United Constitutional Societies of Norwich, who was arrested there and taken into imprisonment in London.

Another SCI member, William Sharpe, was interrogated but released on his agreeing to give evidence for the Crown. Sharpe was a well-known engraver and caused some hilarity at his interrogation by distributing a subscription list to the Privy Councillors for his latest engraving of the Polish freedom fighter Kosciuszko. The incident illustrates the social confidence of the SCI members and the more relaxed atmosphere found at their interrogations. Horne Tooke, for instance, was told that he was being questioned simply to remove any suspicions there might be of his having been involved in treasonable activities. He agreed to answer questions only if he was assured on the gentlemen's honour that there were in fact sworn accusations against him; and since the gentlemen could give him no such assurances the interrogation ended and he was returned to his room in the Tower (which he was beginning to furnish with a range of home comforts). Likewise Joyce refused to answer questions without the presence of his own counsel (which condition was politely refused). When it came to the LCS members, it seems that only Thelwall felt able to resist the probing questions.

This contrast is implied by a *Times* report (20 May 1794) describing the demeanour of the captives:

> Tooke was in high spirits ... and expressed his thanks for the care [taken] of the health of him and his companions; Bonney was also in good spirits; Joyce and Richter were severely and sensibly affected and wept bitterly; Lovatt was confused and stupid; Thelwall was particularly riotous and impertinent, bravadoing everything, and treating every person with contempt.

These events naturally left many LCS members bewildered and fearful. They had lost most of their leading members. There was a reluctance to take on the now vacant offices of secretary and treasurer. Eventually Joseph Burks became secretary. But Ashley was arrested the day after he was elected treasurer, a circumstance that convinced some members that there was a 'rascally spy' in their midst – as indeed there was, though he remained unidentified. A new treasurer could not be found until they hit on the idea of renaming the post 'receiver'. The state of the Society's finances was a continuing worry during the next few months, and this was aggravated by the reduced income as the membership declined. The committee was trying to pay off the £50 they owed their printer, and they had opened subscriptions to support the families of those members who had been arrested. Only gradually did things improve.

The problem of sustaining morale within the Society was still more intractable than these organisational matters. Recruiting virtually dried up. Attendance at the weekly meetings dropped – in August, when the Divisions were asked to vote on the need to revise the Society's constitution, no more than 135 votes were cast. Some Divisions had closed, others with small numbers had united with neighbouring ones, while yet others had 'fallen fast asleep' as the Committee put it.

There were those who proposed that members should now take the oath to 'Live free or die'; others wanted to lie low 'waiting till the Storm be over'. One member 'lamented the Cowardice of Citizens' and a General Meeting was proposed 'to rally the Panic Struck Members'. From Newgate, Gerrald, awaiting transportation, was reported to be 'much dissatisfied with the Society for want of Spirit': he had no doubt that some of those in the Tower would be hanged and 'he supposed the Society would stand by, silent Spectators'.

This was not entirely fair. The Committee of Emergency was discussing a proposal for the publication of a 'Spirited Remonstrance'. This idea was greeted with general approval until it was asked to whom it should be addressed. 'The House of Commons are our Accusers,' it was said. 'We cannot expect that they will hear us with attention. In the House of Lords we have but one solitary friend ... [As to the King] he has not the Power if he had the Will to redress our Wrongs for the Government of this Country is exercised by a Junto of about Twenty Persons'. And yet, it was argued, at least such a Remonstrance would show the country that they had done everything in their power and that if then they resorted to 'other means' it would be clear they were doing so as a 'last Resource'. The discussion was finally ended with John Gale Jones's forthright declaration: 'Shall we remonstrate with those who hold a Knife to our Throats, who have an Axe already whetted and thirst for our Blood? No! Let us in contempt of Death make an appeal to the People and to the People only'.

Thus an eight-page pamphlet was produced, with the somewhat prolix title *An Account of the Seizure of Thomas Hardy, Secretary to the London Corresponding Society, with some remarks on the Suspension of the Habeas Corpus Act*. A description of Hardy's arrest was followed by a refutation of the charges made by the parliamentary Committee of Secrecy. The authors denied that there was any correspondence between the LCS and the French Jacobins, and asserted that the LCS had actually petitioned Parliament for a reform of the House of Commons; they affirmed that their intended Convention was to have been only a means to form a body representative of the whole nation, which would seek the reforms of parliamentary representation which the LCS advocated. While admitting that some LCS members had acquired a knowledge of arms, they explained that this was only in the way encouraged by Alfred the Great – i.e. as a kind of unofficial Home Guard – in case of invasion by Frenchmen, Hessians or Hanoverians.

Jones subsequently proposed that they should publish, in those papers that would accept it, a reaffirmation and explanation of the principles of the LCS, 'in order to show the public at large, that the principles of the Society were not hostile to the Constitution of the Country ...' This was welcomed but unfortunately there was no money to pay for such a publication, and Jones had to find the money himself – though he could afford only a single insertion (in the *Morning Post*).

32

In the tranquillity of rural Lincolnshire, John Cartwright read, perhaps with uncomfortable surprise, of the arrests of some of his friends, and the imputations of treasonable activities levelled at the Society which he had founded. In writing to his wife, who was temporarily away from home, he naturally tried not to betray any great anxiety: 'I saw this morning, by the newspaper, that Hardy and Daniel Adams are apprehended for high treason, and that papers belonging to their societies are to be laid before the House of Commons ... I am smiling to think how my last letter to Adams, if found, will surprise the great ones. They would suspect it to be full of treason, as they might call it; whereas I said that the society, when I last attended it, erred in judgement' – probably a reference to the decision to co-operate with the LCS in planning a Convention.

He would have read also of the battlefields of Europe where the French, emerging from their revolutionary Terror, were beginning to repulse the invading allied armies of 'liberation'. The British navy, however, continued their blockade of the French Atlantic ports and Cartwright would have read with pride (and perhaps with some nostalgic regrets) of the successful engagement of the British ships, led by his old hero Lord Howe, against the French fleet – an event which came to be celebrated as 'the glorious First of June' (it removed the immediate fear of a French invasion), though news of it did not reach London until the 11th and Lincolnshire still later.

Crowds filled the London streets in drunken delight at this victory. It was the custom for householders to signal their patriotic pleasure on such occasions by putting lighted lamps and candles in their windows, and those who failed to do so risked having their unlit windows smashed by the surging rabble. Some of the crowd headed towards the houses of those with reputations of dissent for this very purpose – on this occasion, for instance, Lord Stanhope lost a lot of glass. Another section of the crowd headed down Piccadilly. There are contradictory reports as to whether Mrs Hardy had lit her windows but in any case the mob was not to be deterred from their destructive mission. The poor woman had been sitting in her parlour with only an ageing nurse for company when the noisy hordes gathered outside No.9, smashing her windows, battering on the door and baying for the blood of all traitors. She was trapped. There was no exit at the back, only a small window on the ground floor. Terrified, she called to her neighbours who told her to crawl out through the window. But already six months into her pregnancy, she stuck fast and had to be dragged painfully into the night by her rescuers.

Her husband knew nothing of this till later, though he may have heard the crowds from his little room in the Tower, and wondered and worried. The prisoners were in separate cells, Thelwall next to Hardy, Horne Tooke on the floor below; at first they were in complete isolation, but later they had been allowed to see each other and even exchange a few words during daily exercise on the ramparts. Lydia was permitted two-hour visits twice a week, though all their conversation had to be audible to the warder who sat with them throughout the visit. It was in these conditions, that Thomas heard of his wife's terrifying ordeal.

Ten weeks later Lydia visited her husband for the last time. Soon after leaving him she went into labour. Her child was stillborn. She was left in a weak state, exhausted both by the labour and by the weeks of anxieties. Fearing her life was ebbing, she took her pen to write to Thomas:

My Dear Hardy,

This comes with my tenderest affection for you. You are never out of my thoughts, sleeping or waking. Oh, to think what companions you have with you! None that you can converse with either on temporal or spiritual matters; but I hope the Spirit of God is with you and me and I pray that he may give us grace to look up to Christ. There all the good is that we can either hope or wish for, if we have but faith and patience, although we are but poor sinful mortals. My dear, you have it not in …

At this point she collapsed. The letter was left unfinished and she died soon after. The news was brought to Hardy by his warder. Horne Tooke obtained permission for his doctor, Mr Cline who was regularly attending him, to visit Hardy on the day the news came through, but a stranger was poor comfort for him. He withdrew into himself in melancholy despair. He was convinced that Lydia's death was the result of that terrifying night of 11 June when he, wrenched from her by a brutal government, was unable to protect her. He stayed brooding in his cell for eleven days until Tooke persuaded him to resume his daily exercise, to meet his friends, to lift his spirits so far as he was able. But the bitterness at what seemed to him the callous inhumanity of the agents of his plight never left him.

33

Within two weeks of the death of Mrs Hardy the government had decided to prosecute their prisoners for high treason. This was the most serious crime in the book, and carried with it not just a simple death penalty but the full savagery of hanging, drawing and quartering.

In pronouncing this sentence the judge would ask the Lord to have mercy upon the victim's soul; his body, though, would be granted none. He would be hanged, but cut down while still alive and disembowelled. In all probability this would have finished him off and he would have hardly been conscious to see his entrails being burnt 'before his face'. That done, his head would be severed from his body and the torso cut into four. The King would then decide how the five parts were to be disposed of.

Guy Fawkes and some of his fellow-plotters had suffered this gruesome procedure, but by the end of the eighteenth century the full performance was not really expected. A hanging, and subsequent decapitation, would do. However, the prospect for Hardy and his friends was still one of life or death. But in deciding to play for the highest stakes – treason rather than the lesser crime of seditious libel – the government set themselves a difficult task: they had to prove before a jury that their prisoners had either plotted against the life of the King, or had plotted a war against His Majesty or had allied themselves to the King's enemies. (The fourth possibility – having sexual intercourse with the Queen – was presumably not considered.) Would they be able to establish their reports of pikes and knives and drilling with broomsticks, beyond hearsay, and to demonstrate that these activities were directed against the King? And would they then be able to lay responsibility for these activities at the feet of Hardy or Tooke, or any or all of the others?

The indictment against the twelve men – Hardy, Thelwall, Richter, Moore, Hodgson and Baxter of the LCS, and Horne Tooke, Bonney, Kyd, Joyce, Wardle and Holcroft of the SCI – was put before a Grand Jury to determine whether there was a case to answer. A Special Commission of 'oyer and terminer' (in the quaint terminology of legal mysteries meaning 'to hear and determine') was appointed. It now appeared that the crucial part of the government's case turned on the Convention which the two societies had jointly planned, the intention of which, it was asserted, was either to seize the powers of government (which would have entailed disposing of the King and would therefore have been treasonable), or to intimidate Parliament into gaining their objectives of universal suffrage and annual parliaments. In the latter case it was admitted that there could be some doubt as to whether the action was treasonable, but this should be tested in Court. The Grand Jury agreed there was a case to be put.

So on 13 October the eight in custody (Wardle, Moore, Hodgson and

Holcroft had not been apprehended) were served with indictments. Shortly after this they were transferred under heavy escort to Newgate in readiness for their trials at the Old Bailey, which was situated within this massive prison. The *Morning Post* reported: 'Notwithstanding the great precaution of secrecy, the crowd soon became very great; and the strongest animation of feeling and sympathy was visible in almost every spectator's countenance. Some could not even suppress the expressions of their regard, [but behaved with] the most perfect *real decorum*'. As far as the prisoners were concerned, the *Post* reported that 'they retained all that cheerful fortitude, and even vivacity, which has uniformly characterized them during their confinement; appeared to talk with great gaiety to each other, and to the attendants in the coaches, and bowed and smiled with a gaiety, evidently unaffected, to those who saluted them from the streets and windows'. This spirit of bonhomie had apparently also extended to the prisoners' farewells to their Keepers at the Tower.

But these high spirits did not survive the move to Newgate, which had been re-built after being torn apart in the Gordon riots of 1780. The place was now more heavily fortified, but the prisoners found themselves in far less comfortable quarters than those at the Tower. The cells were more in the nature of dungeons: Horne Tooke recorded that water dripped down the walls of his cell, the floor was wet, the bed damp – not an ideal place for a man of 60, suffering from gout and from urinary and bowel disorders.

One of those not in custody, Thomas Holcroft, was told by a friend who had heard the indictment read that his name was included and advised him to flee the country immediately. But Holcroft put the question to his complex philosophical judgement and decided that he should surrender himself. This turned out not to be as straightforward as might be supposed, since he had great difficulty in convincing Chief Justice Eyre (who was to be the leading judge) that he was in fact the Thomas Holcroft referred to in the indictment. Eventually he was taken off to a Newgate dungeon. But before surrendering himself he had alerted his friend Godwin, who within days had produced a trenchant critique of the Government's case. This was published first in the *Morning Chronicle* and later as a pamphlet under the title *Cursory Strictures on the charge delivered by Lord Chief Justice Eyre to the Grand Jury, Oct 2, 1794*. It was widely read and debated, and may well have influenced the defence that was to be mounted. At the very least it showed that the case was not as clear-cut as might have been supposed.

Meanwhile, as a curtain-raiser, another treason trial was under way in Scotland, part of the aftermath of the Edinburgh convention. Two men, Watt and Downie, were accused of planning an insurrection. Watt, the principal conspirator, had been a government informer, but after the Edinburgh Convention (on which he had reported) he completely changed his loyalties. He conceived a quixotic plan to lure the troops out of Edinburgh Castle at night, and pick them off as they passed through the city, and then to seize the Castle, together with most of the judiciary. The judiciary would then be held as hostages in order to get hold of the treasury, and to force the King to dismiss his Ministers and make peace with the French. A Committee of Ways and Means was formed of which Downie was treasurer. Blacksmiths were engaged to manufacture pikes to be used against the troops. It was these, some of which were discovered by chance in the course of a search of a bankrupt's house, that led to the uncovering of the plot.

At Watt's trial the conspiracy was vaguely linked to the London Corresponding Society by the reading of the minutes of the Edinburgh Convention and an account of the Chalk Farm general meeting of the LCS. Both Watt and Downie were found guilty of treason and sentenced. Downie was later pardoned but Watt was hanged, and though he was excused the prescribed disembowelling and quartering, his head was severed from his corpse and exhibited to the crowd with the usual triumphant formula 'so perish all traitors'.

The stage was now cleared for the main feature. It began at 1 o'clock on the afternoon of Saturday 25 October. The Old Bailey bench was graced by the Lord Mayor of London with six aldermen supporting, and by Chief Justice Eyre and four other judges. Beneath them were the Crown counsel – Sir John Scott (Attorney General), Sir John Mitford (Solicitor General) and no less than six other barristers. Beside all of these, uncomfortably alone, stood John Gurney, junior barrister for the defence, who was forced to explain to the court, once the nine prisoners were brought in, that his principals, Mr Erskine, Mr Gibbs and Mr Vaughan, had been delayed. The Court waited. From the dock Horne Tooke used the hiatus to complain of the draught, contrasting it with the airless, if damp, conditions in his cell.[2] Eyre told him he could return there forthwith if he was ready to plead without the presence of his counsel. Tooke replied that he had seen very little of his counsel, that he had been deprived of his papers and that he had no idea as to what charges were to be brought, but that nevertheless he was quite ready to plead if that was the only way out of this confounded draught. Thelwall too protested at the loss of his papers during the move to Newgate.

Bonney complained of the conditions in which they were being kept 'in which a man can neither sleep by night nor cast his eye on a ray of comfort by day'. Hardy stayed mute. Eyre decided to proceed, calling for the indictment to be read. Erskine and Gibbs crept into court during this reading, in time to hear a lengthy recitation of the alleged acts which the prosecution considered treasonable. At last the prisoners were asked one by one to plead guilty or not guilty: all pronounced themselves not guilty. When asked how they would be tried, all responded with the conventional formula 'By God and my Country' – though Tooke implied that he doubted whether this would be the case.

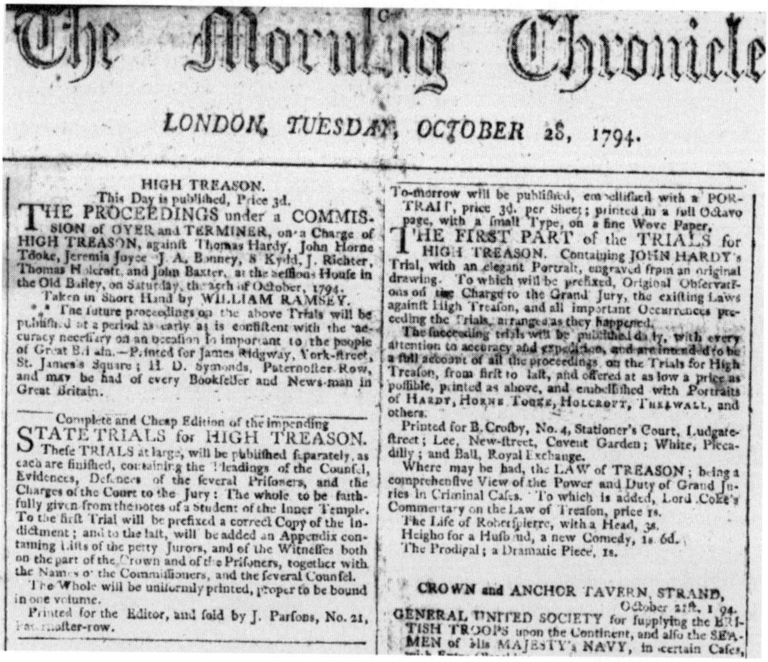

The Morning Chronicle

LONDON, TUESDAY, OCTOBER 28, 1794.

HIGH TREASON.

This Day is publiſhed, Price 3d.

THE PROCEEDINGS under a COMMISSION of OYER and TERMINER, on a Charge of HIGH TREASON, againſt Thomas Hardy, John Horne Tooke, Jeremia Joyce J. A. Bonney, S Kydd, J. Richter, Thomas Holcroft, and John Baxter, at the Seſſions Houſe in the Old Bailey, on Saturday, the 25th of October, 1794.

Taken in Short Hand by WILLIAM RAMSEY.

*** The future proceedings on the above Trials will be publiſhed at a period as early as is conſiſtent with the accuracy neceſſary on an occaſion ſo important to the people of Great Britain.—Printed for James Ridgway, York-ſtreet, St. James's Square; H. D. Symonds, Paternoſter Row, and may be had of every Bookſeller and News-man in Great Britain.

Complete and Cheap Edition of the impending

STATE TRIALS for HIGH TREASON.

Theſe TRIALS at large, will be publiſhed ſeparately, as each are finiſhed, containing the Pleadings of the Counſel, Evidences, Defences of the ſeveral Priſoners, and the Charges of the Court to the Jury: The whole to be faithfully given from the notes of a Student of the Inner Temple. To the firſt Trial will be prefixed a correct Copy of the Indictment; and to the laſt, will be added an Appendix containing Liſts of the petty Jurors, and of the Witneſſes both on the part of the Crown and of the Priſoners, together with the Names of the Commiſſioners, and the ſeveral Counſel.

The Whole will be uniformly printed, proper to be bound in one volume.

Printed for the Editor, and ſold by J. Parſons, No. 21, Paternoſter-row.

To-morrow will be publiſhed, embelliſhed with a PORTRAIT, price 3d. per Sheet; printed in a full Octavo page, with a ſmall Type, on a fine Wove Paper,

THE FIRST PART of the TRIALS for HIGH TREASON. Containing JOHN HARDY's Trial, with an elegant Portrait, engraved from an original drawing. To which will be prefixed, Original Obſervations on the Charge to the Grand Jury, the exiſting Laws againſt High Treaſon, and all important Occurrences preceding the Trials, arranged as they happened.

The ſucceeding trials will be publiſhed daily, with every attention to accuracy and expedition, and are intended to be a full account of all the proceedings on the Trials for High Treaſon, from firſt to laſt, and offered at as low a price as poſſible, printed as above, and embelliſhed with Portraits of HARDY, HORNE TOOKE, HOLCROFT, THELWALL, and others.

Printed for B. Croſby, No. 4, Stationer's Court, Ludgate-ſtreet; Lee, New-ſtreet, Covent Garden; White, Piccadilly; and Ball, Royal Exchange.

Where may be had, the LAW of TREASON; being a comprehenſive View of the Power and Duty of Grand Juries in Criminal Caſes. To which is added, Lord Coke's Commentary on the Law of Treaſon, price 1s.

The Life of Robeſpierre, with a Head, 3s.

Heigho for a Huſband, a new Comedy, 1s. 6d.

The Prodigal; a Dramatic Piece, 1s.

CROWN and ANCHOR TAVERN, STRAND,

October 21ſt, 1794.

GENERAL UNITED SOCIETY for ſupplying the BRITISH TROOPS upon the Continent, and alſo the SEAMEN of His MAJESTY's NAVY, in certain Caſes,

Illustration 3: Extract from the *Morning Chronicle*, 28 October 1794

Erskine, after apologising for his late arrival in court, now requested that the trial be delayed until the following Tuesday to give him time to consult with his clients. This was agreed. The Court would reconvene on 28 October at 7 o'clock in the morning, for the trial of Thomas Hardy.

The speed with which crowds had gathered earlier in the month, to witness the transfer of the prisoners to Newgate, shows the enormous public interest in these trials. Indeed the authorities had clearly feared such a demonstration, and had attempted to effect the move secretly. But word had got out and spread rapidly. Once inside Newgate, the prisoners were seen no more, since the court-room was within the walls. But this did not prevent crowds from assembling outside the gates each day of the trials.

Another indication of this avid public interest were the advertisements that appeared in the papers on the opening day of Hardy's trial, for three separate publications, which promised full accounts of all the trials to be published daily 'at as low a price as possible' (three pence). One of them, was to be 'embellished with portraits'.

34

At 7 o'clock on the morning of Tuesday 28 October, Hardy was again brought to the Old Bailey – the first of the twelve accused to be put in the dock because he was thought to be the most vulnerable. It was after all Hardy who had founded the London Corresponding Society which spearheaded the movement of 'rebellious' societies; he it was who had sent out invitations to the others to join with the LCS in the 'seditious' convention; he had been in correspondence with the pike-makers of Sheffield and perhaps with the hanged traitor Watt. A jury surely could not fail to convict this man, with the mass of evidence which Sir John had assembled; and with Hardy down the other dominoes would inevitably fall.

It took about an hour to select the twelve just and true men from the pool of around two hundred jury-fodder assembled by the Sheriff. Thirty were found to be ineligible, forty-four were challenged by the defence and eight by the Crown before the twelve jurymen were agreed upon and sworn in. They were mostly tradesmen, coal-merchants, brewers, distillers, a biscuit-maker, a mealman; and since they were necessarily freeholders, they were presumably all running their own businesses. There was one gentleman farmer and others whose occupation is not recorded and who would probably have styled themselves 'gentlemen'. It is certain that none of them guessed how arduous a task faced them.

Sir John Scott opened the proceedings with his speech for the Crown. It lasted nine hours – the Lord Chancellor, on hearing this, was said to have commented, 'Nine hours? Then there is no treason, by God!' And indeed, though ostensibly addressing the jury, the Attorney General seemed much of the time to be arguing with himself (or perhaps with Godwin's *Cursory Strictures*). He spent the first two hours delivering a learned monologue on the law of treason, in the course of which he emphasised the need to avoid the use of 'constructive treason' – that is, interpreting motives supposedly implied by certain actions, rather than relying on the evidence of 'overt acts' which were treasonable in themselves.

However, when he proceeded to describe those overt acts he appeared to be in danger of committing the very error he had warned against. The first, and most flagrant, treasonable act, according to Sir John, was the calling of the convention – and he argued that this was not simply a convention, but one 'to be held with intent and in order that the persons to be assembled ... should and might, wickedly and traitorously ... subvert and alter the legislature, rule and government ... and depose the king from the royal state, title, power and government'. Thus the convention was overtly treasonable only through the inclusion of an interpretation of its purposes.

The second overt act was to have 'composed, written, and published divers books, pamphlets, letters, instructions, resolutions, orders, declarations, addresses and writings ... containing incitements, encouragements and exhortations, to move, induce, and persuade the subjects of the king [to send delegates to] not a convention but SUCH a convention ... to be holden for the traitorous purposes before mentioned'.

The final treasonable act was to 'provide arms, of different descriptions, for these purposes ... a conspiracy to make war in the kingdom'. It appears that this was added as a kind of insurance, should the other overt acts not prove sufficiently convincing. For, in explaining this charge, Sir John argued that, 'if you should not be satisfied that the calling [of] such a convention ... was a means to effectuate that compassing and imagination [of the king's death] yet you will find in the evidence even if you pay no attention to that circumstance of calling a convention, sufficient evidence of a conspiracy to depose the king'.

Sir John now proceeded at length to add flesh to the bare bones of the indictment – so much flesh indeed that at times it was difficult to discern the bones beneath. He made sustained efforts to establish a connection between the proposed convention and the National Convention of France which had not only deposed, but had decapitated, their king. He quoted the Addresses which had been sent by both the SCI and the LCS to the French Assembly. He also tried to show that the LCS was inspired by, and had accepted, the ideas of Thomas Paine; and since Paine was an avowed republican this meant that they, too, wanted to see the end of the monarchy.

The candles were lit when Sir John finally sat down. But the jury were given no respite for now the prosecution began its presentation of evidence and as the hours of darkness advanced papers were read, letters, resolutions, addresses, more letters ... As midnight approached, Erskine rose to suggest that maybe the jury was wearying, that although he himself was 'extremely ready' to go on he wondered if the jury were still able to give the matter their full attention. This put the presiding judge, Eyre, into a flutter. Trials in those days were expected to be completed at a single sitting. Could they possibly adjourn? The jury could surely not be allowed to disperse? The Sheriff assured him that beds – or at least, mattresses – could be provided within the building, but Eyre still hesitated. However, when he learnt from the prosecution that they were less than halfway through their evidence, he finally had to relent.

At 8 o'clock on Wednesday morning Hardy was again 'set to the Bar'. The public places quickly filled. The jury, poorly rested after an uncomfortable few hours on the floor, resumed their comfortless seats. The barristers and their clerks reassembled, and all stood as the five judges filed onto the Bench.

The reading of the documentary evidence continued like the relentless drumming of rain. At one point Erskine tried to stem the flood by objecting to the admissibility of a letter written by John Martin to Margarot. How could a letter passing between two people be used as evidence against a third? A protracted legal wrangle followed which ended by all five judges pronouncing against the objection: they considered that the letter could be evidence of a conspiracy in which Hardy was involved. So the deluge of documents continued, now no longer confined to those which the prisoner himself had handled. It was still unfinished when midnight struck.

Before the Court adjourned the jury put in a plea for more restful sleeping quarters and it was conceded that they should be escorted to a hotel in Covent Garden, curiously and onomatopoeically named The Hummums. They were also to be allowed a short sleep-in: the Court would not reconvene until 11 o'clock.

The proceedings resumed on Thursday, with the reading of the constitution of the London Corresponding Society. This was the last piece of documentary evidence. Now some live witnesses were called. Some Sheffield men had been rounded up and after a threatening interrogation about their manufacture of pikes, had agreed to give evidence for the Crown. To quote from the trial transcript:

> Henry Hill sworn. Examined by Mr Law. [A Crown barrister]
> What are you? – A *cutler*. You live at Sheffield? – *Yes* ... Do you know Davison? – *Yes.* He worked for Gale? – *Yes.* Had you an application from Gale to make any blades for pikes? – *Yes.* What orders did he give you respecting the making of them – *Do you mean in the size and number?* In both. – *He brought a bayonet for me as a pattern to make them by, I made one in a bayonet shape, and Davison approved of it* ...To what number did you go on making? – *About a hundred and twenty or a hundred and thirty* [Then referring to possible orders from London] What did you understand to be the purpose for which they were prepared at Sheffield, and which might make them likewise wanted in London? – *To act upon the defensive, in case they should be attacked by an unlawful set of men.* Did Davison say whom they expected would attack them? – *The opposite party that were in Sheffield....*

Hill was able to expand on this point when he was cross-examined by Mr Gibbs for the defence:

> There were some pikes prepared at Sheffield; what was the reason for your preparing them? – *From the opposite party using such threats, even in the dead of night, they have come where I lodged and insulted us of a night when we have been in bed, and have sworn they would pull down the house and burn it, calling us Jacobins, and calling the house Jacobin-house.* – And had you actual reason to expect danger from them? – *Yes, by their threats, they have even shot into peoples houses, an armed set of people that made a parade in the street; and when going home at twelve o'clock at night, they shot under a persons door.*

Another set of people called to the witness box were the government spies who recounted various incidents from the meetings they had attended, highlighting expressions of hostility to the government and to the King, and giving details about the supply of arms. The picture of the Society as a group of desperate characters bent on violent insurrection was becoming well established. But when Erskine came to cross-examine these spies he by-passed their evidence and made it his purpose to expose them as somewhat shady and devious characters. His questioning was at times brutal. Gosling, for instance, had several incidents from his past life brought up which he was obviously reluctant to talk about:

Do you know a Mrs Coleman? – *I do not.* – Look across to the jury? – *I do not know a Mrs Coleman now.* – Did you ever know a Mrs Coleman? – *I did.* – Had you any dealings of any sort with her? – *Certainly, she rented a shop of me.* – Is that all? – *She died at my house, and I buried her.* – Did she leave any will? – *Yes.* – Whom did she leave her property to? – *Her property was left partly to one Burroughs, and partly to one James Leech.* – Who made the will – *I wrote it.*

Gradually Erskine dragged out of him that this James Leech was the son of Gosling's wife, and he went on to plant the implication that Gosling might have forged the will. Then there were questions about the hams filled up with mortar and stones which Gosling had acquired for sale in his wife's shop; and about his dubious dealings in goods from the King's naval stores where Gosling had at one time been employed. Gosling was re-examined by the Crown counsel, Mr Garrow, to give him an opportunity to retrieve his good character; but Erskine had stuck the mud fast.

It now being half-past one o'clock on Friday morning, the transcript-maker records, the Court adjourned until nine o'clock. Through all these proceedings Hardy had sat in the dock, impassive, wordless, watching and listening as the scenes of the last two years were told and mis-told, interpreted and re-interpreted. Letters he had written, documents that he had signed were painted with sinister intentions. Men whom he had trusted were revealed as shabby informers. Each night he was taken back to his dark cell, to his dark dreams. Each morning he was led through the yard where other prisoners exercised. They lined up to watch him pass, many of them calling encouragements; and he would respond 'Farewell citizens! Death or Liberty!' So he resumed his place in the dock, day after day.

More spies were called on Friday morning. Groves first. He described buying knives – *couteaux secrets*, the French name gave them a more sinister ring – from Thomas Green, a hairdresser and perfumier, who was secretive and asked him to keep his voice low lest Mrs Green should hear – she is a damned aristocrat, he had said, according to

Groves. Green, called later, denied this: the knives were openly on sale at any cutler's shop, handy for cutting cheese or meat. 'Very useful', Erskine remarked. 'I will buy one next time I see you'.

The day wore on. About midnight the prosecution launched into some evidence relating to the Edinburgh convention. When this dragged up the case of the condemned, and now executed, traitor Watt, Erskine raised objections as to its relevance. Sir John Scott produced letters purporting to suggest a link between Watt and Hardy. Erskine gave way easily for once, possibly because he had calculated that it would be to his advantage not to prolong the argument, for the end of the Crown's case was in sight and it would be a tactical gain if he could have most of the Saturday sitting for his own speech leaving it in the jury's minds over the Sunday break.

This was just how things worked out.

Illustration 4: The Old Bailey Courtroom from an 1843 engraving

35

Erskine rose to deliver his address at about 1 o'clock on Saturday afternoon. It was a long speech, though a couple of hours shorter than Sir John's; according to Cartwright, who was in court, by the end 'he could not speak loud enough for the judges to hear him ... and an intermediate person was obliged to repeat what he said'. But Erskine was able to hold the Court's attention more surely than had Sir John: he had a more compelling delivery, a more engaging rhetoric, alternating serious exposition with a scathing humour, sincere passion with solemn rationality. He tailored his words to the legal understanding of the judges or to the lay intelligence of the jurors as fitted the occasion. In fact, his speech became famous among the many declarations in support of civil liberty which inspired subsequent reformers. 'This speech will live for ever', wrote Horne Tooke in the margin of his copy of Hardy's trial. Holcroft wrote more publicly, 'Your speech ...was such that every creature who witnessed it, young or old, never mentions it in my hearing but with rapture ... the words you uttered were engraven upon the hearts of your hearers!'

Erskine based his case on a literal interpretation of the law of treason: 'The indictment charges that the prisoners did maliciously and traitorously conspire, and imagine, to bring about and put our lord the King to death'; and that they did this primarily by conspiring 'to cause and bring about a convention'. The charge was not, he emphasised, that they conspired to assemble a convention to depose the King, but that they conspired and compassed his death. 'The prisoner is not charged with a conspiracy against the King's political government, but against his natural life.' This he underlined again and again. 'No act ... of resistance to, or rebellion against the King's regal capacity amounts to high treason ... unless where they can be charged and proved as overt acts in fulfilment of a traitorous intention to destroy the King's natural life.'

Turning to the Crown's evidence, Erskine declared, 'Throughout the whole volumes I have been read, I can trace nothing that even points to the imagination of such a conspiracy'. He ruled out of court whole blocks of evidence such as, for instance, all the matter relating to the Edinburgh convention. 'The charge is not of a conspiracy to hold a convention in Scotland... nor of the part they took in the actual proceedings [there].' Regarding the 'supposed conspiracy' to hold a convention in England: 'This intention therefore is the whole cause – for the charge is not to hold a convention... but the agreement to hold it for the purpose alleged of assuming all the authority of the state and in fulfilment of the main intention against the life of the King.'

But as to conspiracy, 'Not a syllable have we heard read, in the week's imprisonment that we have suffered, that we had not all of us read for months and months before the prosecution was heard of ... It rests with the Crown to show by legal proof that this ostensible purpose [a reform of the House of Commons] was only a cloak to conceal a hidden machination to subvert by force the entire authorities of the kingdom.'

And what of that 'ostensible purpose'? The wisdom of that purpose was beside the point, but the integrity of their intentions might be assessed by referring to others who had put forward a similar case. Erskine cited the 'great Earl of Chatham [the elder Pitt] [who] began and established his fame and glory upon the very cause in which my unfortunate clients were engaged, and he left it as an inheritance to the present minister of the Crown [his son, the younger Pitt] as the foundation of his fame and glory.' And it was on the work of this minister in conjunction with the Duke of Richmond upon which the Constitutional Society was based. 'This plan of the Duke of Richmond was the grand mainspring of every proceeding we have to deal with.' Forget about the 'loose conversations' which have been recounted, he told the jury, these 'extravagances of unknown individuals, not even uttered in the presence of the prisoner'. The proceedings of the Corresponding Society 'appear as following, in form and substance, the plans adopted within our memories, not only by the Duke of Richmond, but by hundreds of the most eminent men of the kingdom'.

He then turned to the more contentious associations that the prosecution had tried to establish. The terms 'convention' and 'delegates', for instance: 'you are desired to believe that [they] were all collected from what had recently happened in France ... But they who desire you to believe this, do not believe it themselves; because they certainly know ... that conventions of reformers were held in Ireland, and delegates regularly sent to them, whilst France was under the dominion of her ancient aristocracy'.

Similarly, he traced the pedigree of the term 'rights of men' which the prosecution had sought to associate with the republican (and hence traitorous) doctrines of Paine. He quoted Burke: 'The rights of men, that is to say the natural rights of mankind, are indeed sacred things ...'

And he referred again to the Duke of Richmond who 'rests the rights of the people of England upon the same horrible and damnable principle of the rights of men'. As for Paine, it was true, Erskine admitted, that 'having imbibed the principle of republican government during the American revolution, he mixed [his argument] with many coarse and harsh remarks upon Monarchy ... But this was collateral to the great object of his work, which was to maintain the right of people to choose their own government'.

This was a risky and daring tactic in the context of the contemporary vilification of Paine, and perhaps only Erskine's eloquence could have made it palatable. In a remarkable passage (which the editor of *State Trials* prints in capitals), Erskine went on to declare his own personal commitment to this interpretation of the rights of man:

I WILL SAY ANYWHERE, WITHOUT FEAR, NAY, I WILL SAY IT HERE, WHERE I STAND, THAT AN ATTEMPT TO INTERFERE, BY DESPOTIC COMBINATION AND VIOLENCE, WITH ANY GOVERN-MENT WHICH A PEOPLE CHOOSE TO GIVE TO THEMSELVES, WHETHER IT BE GOOD OR EVIL, IS AN OPPRESSION AND SUBVERSION OF THE NATURAL AND UNALIENABLE RIGHTS OF MAN; AND THOUGH THE GOVERNMENT OF THIS COUNTRY SHOULD COUNTENANCE SUCH A SYSTEM, IT WOULD NOT ONLY BE STILL LEGAL FOR ME TO EXPRESS MY DETESTATION OF IT, AS I HERE DELIBERATELY EXPRESS IT, BUT IT WOULD BECOME MY INTEREST AND DUTY.

But for Erskine this was by no means the end of his marathon speech: he now moved to other pieces of evidence the crown lawyers had presented. There was, for instance, a crucial reply to a letter from the Norwich societies, who had wanted to know where the LCS really stood – was it still satisfied with the Duke of Richmond's plan or did it intend to rip up the monarchy by its roots and place democracy in its stead [as they thought the Manchester society seemed to want]? The LCS had responded with what the prosecution alleged was ambiguous language, concealing their real aim – the total destruction of the monarchy. But Erskine maintained that the LCS reply bore none of the crown's interpretation. It had urged the people of Norwich to 'put monarchy, democracy and even religion quite aside ... Let your endeavours go to increase the numbers of those who desire a full and equal representation of the people, and to have a Parliament, so chosen, to reform all existing abuses; and if they don't answer at the year's end you may choose others in their stead'. Contrary to the Attorney General's assertion that this was but 'lamely expressed', Erskine saw it as an explicit reaffirmation of the Richmond plan and a reliance on supremacy of parliament.

Erskine then turned to the evidence, mainly about pikes and pistols, presented by the spies and informers. With evident relish, he vilified that treacherous trade, quoting again from Burke: 'The mercenary informer [sows] the seeds of destruction in civil intercourse ... [and has] a tendency to degrade and abase mankind, and to deprive them of that assured and liberal state of mind which alone can make us what we ought to be ...' With this testimonial in mind, Erskine turned to the first of this tribe, Mr Alexander, who, in cross-examination 'stood stammering, not daring to lift up his countenance – confused – disconcerted – and confounded'. Then 'driven from the accusation of pikes ... [we were left with] this miserable, solitary knife held up to us as the engine which was to destroy the constitution of this country'. The spy Groves was treated in similarly scathing terms. 'He tells you he attended at Chalk Farm: and there, forsooth, amongst about seven or eight thousand people he saw two or three persons with knives'. As to the evidence of Lynam, 'it destroys itself by its own intrinsic inconsistency ... It lasted, I think, about six or seven hours, but I have marked passages so grossly contradictory, matter so impossible ... [which will] destroy the rest.'

Erskine concluded his long speech with a warm reference to Hardy's integrity.

> Whatever irregularities or indiscretions they [the LCS] might have committed, their purposes were honest; – and that Mr Hardy's, above all other men, can be established to have been so ... I will show his character to be religious, temperate, humane, and moderate, and his uniform conduct all that can belong to a good subject, and an honest man.

Now exhausted and barely audible, this great advocate sat down. The Court adjourned for an hour and a half 'for refreshment'. The editor of *State Trials* adds in a footnote:

> So strongly prepossessed were the multitude in favour of the innocence of the prisoner, that when Mr Erskine had finished his speech, an irresistible acclamation pervaded the Court, and to an immense distance round. The streets

were seemingly filled with the whole of the inhabitants of London and the passages were so thronged that it was impossible for the judges to get to their carriages. Mr Erskine went out and addressed the multitude, desiring them to confide in the justice of the country...

This note was probably written some time after the event and is not entirely accurate. Press reports at the time suggest that the crowds, hearing the applause from within the Court, assumed it meant that Hardy had been acquitted. Erskine addressed the multitude on a later occasion (see chapter 37).

36

After the adjournment, at about eight o'clock in the evening, Erskine's co-counsel, Mr Gibbs, started the presentation of the defence evidence with a long procession of witnesses attesting to the character of the prisoner. Alexander Fraser, tailor: *'An unblemished character'*. William Barclay, shoemaker (Hardy's employer for seven years): *'A very good character ... as quiet as a man can be'*. John Carr: *'A sober, honest, worthy man'*. John Stevenson, coal-merchant: *'A man of mild, peaceable disposition ... he always behaved with great uprightness ... and as to moral character, I know of no man that goes beyond him'*. Alexander Gregg, book-binder: *'Always a very sober, industrious, rather a religious man'*. Peter Macbean, shoemaker: *'A very amiable character indeed, both civil and religious ... A peaceable, quiet, well-disposed man'*. And so on. Two dissenting ministers added their endorsements to these testimonials: the Reverend James Stevens of the chapel which Hardy attended affirmed that *'His character, in our congregation, is much to his honour as to his moral conduct and as being a peaceable member of a christian society and he is believed by all in that society to be a man of conscience, both towards God and man'*. The Reverend Thomas Oliver described how he had struck up an acquaintance with Hardy when sheltering in a doorway from a shower of rain. *'I found him very agreeable'*, said the minister, who subsequently became a regular visitor at the Hardys' home, and enjoyed many interesting conversations, some relating to the reform of parliament. *'I believe that he is one that fears God and honours the King'*. This last remark was seized upon by the Attorney-General in his cross-examination of the unfortunate minister, confronting him with LCS resolutions in favour of Paine's *The Rights of Man*. 'Does this show the sort of man that you would suppose honours the King?' Sir John thundered. The Reverend faltered: '*I have but very little time to meddle with such matters ... I have four sermons to preach in a week, and as I make them myself I have very little spare time*'.

The questioning and cross-questioning continued until half-past one on Sunday morning, when the court at last adjourned until eight o'clock on Monday morning. The throng outside had still not dispersed. According to the *Morning Post* of 3 November 1794: 'Upon Mr Erskine's entering his carriage, the crowd ... wishing to express their sense of his extraordinary and brilliant exertions upon this day immediately took the horses from his carriage and drew him home. They then separated, with reiterated exclamations, 'ERSKINE FOR EVER!'

Hardy's ordeal had still another two days to run, but he must have returned to his cell with a rather easier mind and greater hope than at any other point during the preceding week.

On Monday morning the evidence for the defence continued. It was established that among the papers which the King's messenger had found in Hardy's house at the time of his arrest was the letter from Sheffield offering to supply arms to the people of Norwich. It was intended that Hardy should have forwarded this letter to Norwich but in fact it was found unopened and unsent. A number of LCS members were called to attest to the Society's adherence to the Duke of Richmond's plan for reform and to the intention of obtaining these reforms by constitutional means. This was corroborated by Daniel Stuart, secretary to the committee of the very respectable Society of Friends of the People, who spoke of his friendship with Hardy and of their many discussions about parliamentary reform. The Duke of Richmond himself was called and his long *Letter to Col Sharman*, in which his famous plan was spelled out, was read. The renowned playwright turned politician, Richard Sheridan, took the witness stand to testify to his belief that the LCS was wedded to constitutional means to obtain their desired reforms. The Earl of Lauderdale too added his voice to the same effect.

At last Mr Gibbs rose to sum up the case for the defence. At the end of his speech the Lord Chief Justice addressed the prisoner: 'Mr Hardy... you are at full liberty to speak for yourself if you wish to do so, and if you do, this is the proper time for you to be heard'.

This elicited Hardy's second contribution to the proceedings: 'My Lord,' he said, 'I am perfectly satisfied with the defence my Counsel have made for me, and I apprehend that there is no need for me to say more.'

Lord Eyre: 'And you do not wish to add anything?'

Mr Hardy: 'No, my Lord.'

So the Solicitor General (Sir John Mitford) rose to sum up for the prosecution, which he did at some length. Indeed, he was still speaking three hours later when the Court adjourned at twenty minutes past midnight. He continued for another five hours the following day. Only then was the Court allowed to hear the summing up by the Lord Chief Justice. This was felt to be crucial to the final outcome and weary as they must have been the twelve jurymen, and of course, Hardy himself would have turned their flagging attention to his words with renewed interest. Lord Eyre did not spare them. He spoke through the rest of the day and half of the following one, Wednesday.

The Judge's summing up was generally acknowledged to be fair. He observed that 'conspiring to depose the King and to subvert the monarchy ... has always been considered as an overt act of the treason of compassing the death of the King'. But he agreed with the counsel for defence that the proof of such conspiring ought to be 'clear and convincing'. The question then resolved itself as to whether 'the prisoner and other persons have conspired to subvert the monarchy and whether they have set on foot a project of a convention of the people in order to effect it'. He agreed that Hardy had set out originally upon the Duke of Richmond's plan: 'the prosecution have to satisfy you that they have departed from that plan into a criminal pursuit of another object ... the establishment of a government by a representation of the people only: a pure democracy.'

Lord Eyre turned to the historical development of the London Corresponding Society from its obscure birth in 1792. He referred the jury to the correspondence with Norwich regarding the LCS attitude to the Lords and to the Monarchy. He had the letters re-read, cautioning the jury against seeking 'much niceness of critical inquiry to fix the meaning' of the words. They should expect a clear avowal of intention. If the LCS had not departed from the Duke of Richmond's plan, there should be no equivocation. There was more than a suspicion that the judge detected no such avowal – but of course it was for the jury to decide.

He then turned to the LCS Address to the French National Assembly and asked the jury to consider whether the prosecution was right in their assertion that this Address and its manner of presentation by the LCS agent demonstrated an avowal of republicanism. Again, the judge seemed to think ... but it was for the jury to decide.

Likewise he drew attention to various resolutions 'importing warm and unqualified approbation' of the writings of Thomas Paine. The LCS not only approved of his works but 'they dispersed them all over the country, with a wonderful anxiety and at great expense'. The prosecution averred that this demonstrated an attachment to republicanism. The defence maintained that it was their attachment to those parts which defend the rights of man – to which there could be no reasonable objection. But in this case, the judge asked 'was it not the duty of honest men, of good subjects ... to have taken some pains to have separated the bad parts from the good?' They did no such thing; and 'that the publications must have [done] a great deal of mischief by alienating the minds of the King's subjects from his person and government and from the constitution, is perfectly clear'. But, he added, 'how much of this effect these persons intended, I shall leave entirely for your consideration'.

The outlook must have appeared bleak to Hardy at this stage as he listened from the dock to the Lord Chief Justice. Any euphoria that his counsel's defence may have stimulated must have been sadly deflated. But his face remained impassive as ever.

However towards the end of his summing up, Lord Eyre seemed to find more in favour of the prisoner. He more or less dismissed all the evidence about arms. 'I should have thought,' he said, 'no great reliance was to be laid upon it.' He instructed the jury 'to attend, and to attend with favour, to everything that can be urged on the part of the prisoner'. His defending counsel had not tried to deny his part in the proceedings of the LCS. 'He was the promoter, designer and inventor of some of the measures.' But they say that 'he is a plain man, of great simplicity of manners, peaceable and orderly in his deportment, and a friend to the constitution of his country; having one great political object in his mind, namely, the obtaining a radical reform in the Commons House of Parliament, by the introduction of universal suffrage and annual elections...'

Half an hour after noon the jury withdrew. They refused refreshments offered, even though they were warned that none could be provided once they had begun their deliberations. Perhaps they expected only a short discussion; perhaps they wished not unnecessarily to prolong the prisoner's agonising uncertainty; perhaps they simply wanted to get home as soon as possible after their twelve days' confinement.

It was, however, three hours before they returned to court to pronounce Hardy 'not guilty of the high treason whereof he stood indicted'. At this the prisoner made the third pronouncement of his long ordeal. He said, 'My fellow countrymen, I return you my thanks'.

And so Hardy was discharged.

37

The not-guilty verdict had been received 'with a murmur of Joy' (according to the *Morning Post* report the next day). This murmur 'soon reached the People without doors, whose acclamations rent the air'. The crowd, which had assembled outside the Old Bailey for several nights past, had swelled considerably since the rumour had spread that the jury was out. Now they waited to glimpse the principals of this twelve-day drama.

There is no report of the members of the jury having been recognised as they left to regain the peace of their homes. But they were not ignored by the Press.

> What must be the consolation of the twelve Jurymen on their return to society! Cut off from all intercourse with the world for nine days, they were unacquainted with the lively interest which the public took in the issue of the cause; they knew not that there was a pause in all the general concerns of life ... Now what must be their sensations on finding that their verdict has given to every independent spirit in England the most rapturous satisfaction! And that they are welcomed back to the bosom of their Country as the Saviours of its Constitution!

As to the two heroes of the defence:

> Mr Erskine and Mr Gibbs, whose glorious struggle upon this occasion will make them ever dear to mankind, were eager to avoid the burst of gratitude that they must expect from the multitude. They continued a very considerable time in the Court after the acquittal; but the vigilance and patience of gratitude were not to be wearied. They were recognized and conducted in triumph to Sergeant's Inn...'[4]

From there it seems Erskine proceeded home though still accompanied by the throng. The *Morning Post* (6 November 94) reported that: 'he appeared at his dining-room window and addressed the People. After thanking them for the honour they had given him, and expressing his satisfaction at 'the honest Verdict of your Countrymen [that] has assured Englishmen that they have yet the Liberty of Speech'. He appealed to the crowd to 'peaceably return to your respective homes, and that whatever your feelings may be on the acquittal of a guiltless fellow countryman that they will not hurry you beyond the bounds of moderation and decorum, as many friends to the prosecution and enemies to public justice would be happy to take advantage of any honest manifestations of joy which they may construe into tumult and disorder. Let me urge you to temperance – for this is a proud day for Britain – and therefore let us retire in peace, and Bless God'.[5]

Cries of 'Erskine forever!' greeted this speech and in less than a quarter of an hour every part of Fleet Street was cleared.

There were of course many of Hardy's friends amongst the crowd outside Newgate waiting to greet their hero. But he was in no mood to face their raucous joy. He had been imprisoned for seven months. Now he had no home. His wife was dead. His children had all perished. He would have preferred to walk alone through the London streets, musing on the sweetness of his liberty and on the bitterness of his bereavement.

He found his way to a back gate of the prison and stepped into the free air of the evening. But he was soon spotted and taken to a waiting carriage. The horses had been loosed from the shafts so that the carriage could be drawn by his friends.

> They drew him in a coach to his house in Piccadilly, making the tour of Pall-mall and St James's Street. He had been thus hurried along by the enthusiastic zeal of the multitude, and it was at length with difficulty that he was able to tell them that he was desirous of going to the house of his brother-in-law, in Lancaster Court in the Strand. He was drawn thither, and having got out of the carriage, before he entered the house, he went into the Church-yard of St Martin and was shown to the grave of his Wife, from whose side he had been taken when first seized and who had fallen under the shock. The multitude respected this feeling with a sympathy that did them credit. – They kept at a distance while his relation pointed out the grave. After this affecting scene, he went into his brother's house, and in a short address thanked his Fellow-countrymen for the kind interest they had shewn

in his favour, and he requested them, as they valued the cause in which they had displayed their zeal, that they would separate in peace ...

The cry of 'home, home!' was given, and in three minutes the multitude quietly dispersed.[6]

The *Morning Post* carried a similar report and added that the controlled behaviour of the crowd showed 'what we have always endeavoured to inculcate, that the Friends of Freedom are the Friends of Peace and Order'. But of course not everyone greeted the acquittal with joy. *The Times*, for instance, reported none of these euphoric scenes except by implication. 'Let the Public rejoice that a fellow-creature (in whose conduct, however reprehensible in other respects, the Jury did not find what amounted to a confirmed act of High Treason) is saved from an ignominious death'. It was convinced that the government had been wise and vigilant in bringing the case to judgement, for 'that these Societies were formed for purposes very different from what they professed, is a truth which the evidence brought forward against HARDY has proved beyond all contradiction'. So he was lucky to get away with his life and *The Times* advised him not to meddle any more in these matters.

Clearly it rankled that a man from the lower reaches of society should have presumed to interfere in the affairs of state, and in what was evidently intended as a witty conclusion for readers to chuckle over, Hardy was put in his place:

As the shoemaker has been HARDY enough to take compleat measure of the laws of England, we hope he will now be sufficiently master of where the shoe pinches, and pare his political leather with a more constitutional instrument than a PIKE. Let him keep to the old adage '*ne sutor ultra crepidum*' [usually loosely translated as 'Let the cobbler stick to his last']: and then he may make both ends meet, without coming to an untimely end at the LAST!

38

Cartwright sat through Hardy's ordeal with some impatience, waiting his turn on the witness stand at Tooke's trial which was scheduled to follow. This was in a sense a trial of Cartwright's own Society for Constitutional Information. He had worked with Tooke over the years, whereas he had never even met Hardy, and had evinced no particular interest in the London Corresponding Society. He may even have had some sympathy with the Government's case against some of the reported activities of LCS members, who were working men, like those on his Lincolnshire estate whom he treated so unsympathetically. On the other hand he was certainly outraged at the wholesale arrests and treason charges: 'The trials will, I think, turn out as I always expected, vindictive and iniquitous...' So when he wrote to his wife at the end of Hardy's trial, 'I need not tell you the heart-felt joy which the words "Not Guilty" gave me', his satisfaction was probably more to do with the prosecution's failure and the hope it gave to his friend Tooke than with the vindication of the LCS or Hardy's escape from the scaffold.

Even after Hardy had been discharged, Cartwright had another twelve days to wait before Tooke's trial started. Erskine and Gibbs were again engaged for the defence, assisted this time by Tooke's nephew, Felix Vaughan. The Attorney General, Sir John Scott, and the Solicitor General, Sir John Mitford led the prosecution with seven other barristers in attendance. Chief Justice Eyre reappeared with his retinue of judges and justices.

As soon as Tooke had been 'set to the bar' he asked to be seated with his counsel rather than in the dock. He had been unable, he said, to instruct his counsel and he feared that, judging by the course of Hardy's trial, 'whole passages of my life' were to be brought into question which it was impossible for his counsel to know anything about. It was, he claimed, 'my right by law ... to be placed in that situation which is best adapted for my defence'. Tooke, with some reason, fancied himself as a lawyer and the denial of his right to practice (probably because his abrasive arrogance which had made him enemies within the profession) still rankled. Now was his chance to exhibit the talent the law had lost: he would defend himself! And it seems that Erskine, though determined to remain in control of the defence team, was not unwilling for Tooke to play a part. But Eyre demurred, and only after a lengthy argument did he concede that the court would indulge him on account of his ill health. Tooke had achieved his objective even if not the whole argument. He took his privileged place beside Erskine and Gibbs with satisfaction.

That little tussle resolved, it was time to the select of the jury. The prosecution ruthlessly objected to any candidate whom they deemed not likely to be sympathetic to the Crown's case, and by the time nine men had been selected Erskine (according to Cartwright) said to

Tooke, 'By God they are murdering you'. However, by then the prosecution had used up their permitted number of unqualified objections and, rather than making a case against the subsequent candidates, they allowed the last three to be empanelled without further argument. Even so, it looked to the defence a very hostile jury.

The main thrust of Tooke's defence was to show that, whatever might be said of others (and Hazlitt commented, perhaps unkindly, that he 'rather compromised his friends to screen himself'), he had always been moderate in his aspirations for reform, for ever restraining the excesses of others; that he was a loyal and supportive subject of the King and a firm upholder of the constitution. Indeed, this was not far from the truth. 'His politics were not at all revolutionary', says Hazlitt, adding somewhat viciously, 'In this respect he was a mere pettifogger, full of chicane, and captious objections, and unmeaning discontent.' His contention of moderation was behind his somewhat overworked image of the stage-coach from which he insisted he would alight at Hounslow, even though others stayed on to Windsor.

Cartwright explained this metaphor in his customary prosaic fashion during his cross-examination by Erskine. Was Tooke 'a man floating between different opinions, taking up one opinion one day and another on another?' – 'Of all men I ever knew', declared Cartwright, 'Mr Tooke appeared to me to be the steadiest and most invariable in his opinions...' – 'Did you ever hear anything fall from him disrespectful of the office of royalty in this country?' – 'Quite the reverse ... I have always heard him maintain that the regal and the aristocratical branches of the constitution of this country were good and excellent in themselves, and that if a reform of the other branch of the constitution, meaning the House of Commons, could be obtained, that our constitution then, in his opinion, would be the most perfect of any upon earth ...' and now Cartwright seized the opportunity to deliver his lecture on the subject of Tooke's stage-coach metaphor.

> I can recollect a conversation, I believe two or three times repeated [!] ... a sort of illustration that Mr Tooke made use of, in order to show that his objects did not go the same lengths as those of Mr Paine and other persons who speculated upon government: I remember particularly his illustrating it by speaking of persons travelling in a stage-coach together: he said, men may get into the same stage-coach with an intention of travelling a certain distance: one man chooses to get out at one stage, another at another; and so some men may want something more than a reform – I want a reform of

the House of Commons only. And, still pursuing his simile of the stage-coach, he said – If I and several men are in the Windsor stage, when I find myself at Hounslow, I get out; they who want to go further, may go to Windsor or where they like; but when I get to Hounslow (applying it to the House of Commons) there I get out; no further will I go, by God.

Cartwright's most awkward moments came when the Attorney General cross-examined him. He had to admit to his own extensive ignorance owing to his absence from London of much of the SCI's more recent proceedings: he had no first-hand knowledge of the Addresses to France, of the Society's correspondence with the Norwich society, nor of the letter which the SCI had sent to Sheffield periodical the *Patriot*, 'in which it was stated that the vipers, Monarchy and Aristocracy, are writhing under the grasp of the Infant Freedom'. The Attorney General pressed him: 'Do you remember any conversation in which this phrase was used?' – 'I do not remember such a conversation.' And if he had 'you would have been vastly surprised, should you not?' – 'It would depend on the circumstances ...' – 'Do you mean to say it would not have surprised you?' Sir John asked, incredulously. 'If it had applied to any government where Monarchy and Aristocracy had been vipers to Freedom, I should have thought it well applied.' And if it had been applied to the English monarchy? Cornered, Cartwright continued to squirm: 'That is a general question to which it is very difficult to give a clear and satisfactory answer ...' Sir John felt no need to press the point further.

Charles Fox, then Whig Leader, was called to be examined by Erskine, mainly on the subject of the so-called Thatched House Tavern meeting which had been called in 1785 by Wyvill, whose group of Yorkshiremen had wanted a reform of the parliamentary constituencies so as to protect their business interests (see chapter 10). The object of this meeting had been to rally support for Pitt, who was about to introduce a reform Bill into the House of Commons, though the reforms were of such an innocuous nature that the real aim of the Thatched House meeting seems to have been to head off the more radical reformers from opposing the Bill for its inadequacies.

Tooke's defence thought to use accounts of his supportive role during this meeting to demonstrate his moderate intentions. Unfortunately, Fox's memory of the occasion turned out to be somewhat hazy and when the Duke of Richmond was called it appeared that his memory was even worse. Tooke himself had taken over the examination of his Grace and was patiently persistent in the face of gallingly frustrating responses. 'My own recollection does not serve me on this occasion ...' – 'It has escaped my memory ...' – 'I have some faint recollection of that, but ...' – 'I am very sorry but I cannot recollect it ...' – 'It is very possible that such a thing was said to me, but I do not recollect it ...' The Duke could not even be sure that Tooke had been present at the meeting: 'I have several times seen Mr Horne Tooke at public places, but whether exactly at the London Tavern or the Thatched House ... I cannot charge my memory to the exact places.'

It is therefore no surprise to find that Eyre confided shortly afterwards that he had 'put a mark against the whole of that [the Duke's evidence] in my notes – that it amounts to nothing'. When Pitt himself was called, Tooke had no greater success: he failed to persuade Eyre that the evidence concerning a letter written by Pitt to some third person was admissible evidence, since Tooke himself was not involved in the exchange. So Tooke was obliged to abandon his hopes for help from this important witness – which had been sanguine hopes in any case, since Pitt was the chief instigator of the indictment against him.

The prosecution's case covered much of the ground that had featured in Hardy's trial, though the emphasis was naturally on the activities of the SCI rather than the LCS. But it also tried to show that Tooke had played a crucial role in aiding and abetting the LCS and other working-men's societies. There was for instance the unfortunate – from Tooke's point of view – matter of the signature at the end of the LCS's first Address to the nation. What had happened was that, because of his inexperience at that time, Hardy had sent the draft of the Address to Tooke for vetting. Tooke had made some minor alterations and then added Hardy's name, as the Society's secretary, and sent it to the printers. The original document was produced in court and there was no denying Tooke's hand. In fact he made no attempt to deny it, preferring to explain the, to him, innocent circumstances. But the prosecution used this to suggest that Tooke had virtually created, and certainly manipulated, the LCS. (Throughout the trial Tooke was always ready to admit his own hand and sought to save the prosecution the laborious trouble of finding an independent witness to verify it. For, he said, 'I have never done an action, never written a sentence in public or in private, I have never entertained a thought on any political subject, which I have the smallest hesitation to admit.')

In his summing up, Eyre dealt at great length and very seriously with the Scottish convention, to which the SCI had sent a delegate (Sinclair), and the planning of the English convention in which the SCI had collaborated with the LCS. As in Hardy's trial, the prosecution had sought to demonstrate that these conventions had aimed not simply to reform parliament but to usurp the functions of government. Eyre appeared to take this interpretation very seriously. (Had he been privately admonished for his treatment of this issue at Hardy's trial?) 'One can hardly believe', he now said, 'that a parliamentary reform of the House of Commons was the object. One must suspect that more was intended; but the question is, what more was intended ...'. Not that Tooke was directly involved; but he did chair the SCI meetings when arrangements were being discussed. And 'when there is a rebellion, every man in it is involved', though usually, Eyre added ominously, 'the leaders are selected for example'.

On the other hand he agreed that Tooke had demonstrated in his examinations of witnesses, that on many occasions through the 1780s he had declared his attachment to the constitution, to the sharing of government by the King, the aristocracy and the Commons. And he had witnesses to testify that his way of life – his scholarly devotion to books, his fondness of his garden, his withdrawal, on account of his poor health, from society – made it seem that he 'would, in truth, be the last man in England that could be justly suspected of being engaged in a conspiracy of this kind.' And yet, and yet ... 'he is found dealing in these subjects by his intercourse with Hardy, by his interference with the papers of the society [the LCS] ... by that unfortunate publication [referring to] 'those vipers, Monarchy and Aristocracy...'

Eyre was evidently unsure as to what the proper outcome of the trial should be, and he concluded his summing up with a confession of the tension between his instinctive sympathies and his professional rationality: 'I wish heartily that Mr Tooke had put this case really beyond all suspicion, because I see, with great regret, a man of his cultivated understanding, of his habits, of his capacity to be useful to mankind ... But I cannot say that he has done so. There is certainly a great deal to be explained.'

The jury retired at about eight o'clock on the evening of 22 November, after six long days in court. But, for all their apparent, or perceived, bias at the beginning of the trial, they now seemed to share none of the judge's uncertainties. They returned after only eight minutes to declare Tooke 'Not Guilty'. The government had lost another round.

39

Tooke's acquittal was greeted 'by almost every person in Court with acclamations, and shouts of joy and congratulations ... The roar, or rather convulsive screams of joy, lasted, without cessation for several minutes – The cheering sound was soon caught by the attendant Populace without, on whom it had an electrical effect; for the air was instantly resounded with the loudest acclamation of joy.'[7]

Once the applause had subsided, Tooke leapt to his feet and began to deliver, in contrast to Hardy's single-liner, a rather lengthy speech. First he thanked the Lord Chief Justice and then the gentlemen of the jury for their fairness and patience during 'this tedious trial'. (He later confided to his friends that were he to be charged with treason again he would immediately plead guilty rather than having to endure another speech from the Solicitor-General.) His speech had hardly begun when part of the gallery collapsed. This naturally caused no little commotion but Tooke was not one to be deterred by any such mishap: he waited for the disturbance to subside and then resumed his important communication. Despite the verdict, he was apparently anxious to dispel any doubts about his involvement, and with good reason it seems. It was not long before Hardy was being referred to as an 'acquitted felon' in a Commons debate: a not-guilty verdict, William Windham explained, did not necessarily imply innocence, merely the absence of a *legal proof* of guilt. Pitt went even further, declaring that the juries' verdicts only demonstrated how right the government had been in supposing that the rot of subversion had penetrated deep.

Tooke concluded his speech with a challenging taunt at his accusers. 'I am glad I have been prosecuted,' he said, 'and I hope this will make the Attorney General more cautious in future. He said he would have no treason by construction, and there is no suspicion against me but by construction and inference'. But this was, in fact, perilously close to Windham's equivocation.

With the case now concluded, Tooke was free to enjoy, with none of Hardy's ambivalence, the triumphant welcome that awaited him in the streets outside. Later that evening he dined with about twenty of his friends, including Major Cartwright. Some days later Tooke entertained again at his home in Wimbledon, and it happened that the Home Minister Dundas, who lived next door to Tooke, was having a dinner-party at the same time, with Pitt among the guests. Cartwright wrote to his wife the next day: 'We drank the King's health which I daresay was not suspected at the next door'.

On the following day, 1 December, John Bonney, Jeremiah Joyce, Stewart Kyd and Thomas Holcroft, the members of the SCI still in custody, were brought to the bar at the Old Bailey. A new jury having been sworn in, the Attorney General said that in view of the recent acquittals he did not intend to submit any evidence against these four and they were dismissed. And so half of the twelve apostles, as they came to be known, were restored to liberty.

Three remained in the cells of Newgate, all members of the LCS.[8] They were not released because the government still had hopes that the next trial – that of Thelwall – would turn out differently. But these last hopes were dashed too. Erskine led for the defence again, and had to contend with all the evidence that the prosecution had adduced from the colourful language of his client's public lectures and speeches. Erskine could not trust Thelwall not to hang himself with more impetuous indiscretions, and so did not allow him the same freedom he had given Tooke to participate in his own defence. It turned out that the trial ran a mere four days, however, although the jury needed three hours before agreeing on yet another acquittal.

The government had no option now but to set the remaining prisoners free and to shred the warrants they had prepared for the arrest of another six hundred (so it was said) conspirators up and down the country.

NOTES

1. Quotations from *Times*, 17 May 1794.
2. Quotations in this and subsequent sections are taken from the transcripts reproduced in *State Trials*.
3. *Morning Chronicle*, 7 November 1794.
4. *Morning Chronicle*, 7 November 1794.
5. *Morning Post*, 6 November 1794.
6. *Morning Chronicle*, 6 November 1794.
7. *Morning Post*, 24 November 1794.
8. Curiously, three of those named in the indictment – Thomas Wardle (an SCI member), Richard Hodgson and Matthew Moore – had never been arrested. They had not hidden: in fact Hodgson had on one occasion tried to surrender himself, but the magistrates had gone to lunch!

PART IV ENDINGS

40

Once the euphoric crowds had dispersed, having seen Hardy disappear into his brother-in-law's house, he was left to piece together the scattered fragments of his life. Not for him the comforts of home, or the merry parties which Tooke enjoyed: he had no home, no family, no means of support. He was in poor health, and his friends were reported to be fearful for his life, though there is no mention of this in his own *Memoir*.

A week after his acquittal he wrote a thank-you letter which filled a column of the *Morning Post*. He surely felt a deep relief and gratitude to those who had helped him – his LCS comrades, Erskine and Gibbs, the supportive public, the jurymen – but he had never been a great communicator and his feelings were masked in this letter by an awkward formality. He ended with a paragraph explaining his own difficult circumstances. 'I find my business ruined and I have to begin the World again'. Having announced that as soon as he could find suitable premises he intended to open a shop once more, he concluded, 'I have no doubt of receiving that encouragement and support, which injured Innocence never yet has failed to obtain, in this generous and liberal Island.'

Never yet? Had he forgotten the unrelieved poverty to which this 'generous and liberal island' had consigned those about him? Or the privations for whose amelioration he had been working and indeed risking his life? In his *Memoir* he had a different tale to tell: there he wrote that after his trial he 'formed a resolution of bidding an everlasting adieu to a country where he had been thus maltreated ... where he saw the most exalted virtues treated as the greatest crimes'. He determined to 'expatriate himself', to emigrate to America, the new republic where he had 'many flattering offers'.

Illustration 5: A London Street near where Hardy established his business in 1797 (see section 44)

Perhaps to his later regret, he allowed his many friends to dissuade him from this resolve, and towards the end of November he opened his new shop at No 36 Tavistock Street in Covent Garden. At first business was brisk. His shop was filled 'from morning to night' and in the street outside 'crowds collected about the door and windows out of curiosity to see him'. He had to employ a man simply to take and record the measurements of the many feet that were to be shod. The cobbler had returned to his last, as *The Times* had so patronisingly advised.

Major Cartwright was one of those to place an order, telling him that 'no man but himself should ever make him a pair of shoes so long as either of them lived' – a promise Cartwright strictly adhered to, according to his niece, until Mr Hardy retired from business. But not all his patrons were so faithful. After a few weeks public curiosity was sated, the crowds receded, and in two or three months Hardy found his custom tailing off so that whereas he was at one point employing as many as six journeymen, this number was soon reduced to two, and later to one. In fact by the summer of 1795 his business was so slack that he decided to take time off for a short tour of the Midlands, to Northampton, Leicester, Nottingham and Derby, visiting people he had corresponded with as Secretary of the LCS. It appeared that he was still something of a celebrity in the provinces and he found himself 'kindly and hospitably treated by some of the principal people' in these towns.

Apart from the ephemeral nature of public memory, no less so then than now, there was another reason for the decline in Hardy's custom. It was rumoured that he was being generously supported by a number of rich sympathisers. It was said that he was living rent-free, that he was receiving an annuity from some unnamed nobleman, that more than one gentleman had willed him legacies. These were false rumours though not entirely groundless. The Earl of Lauderdale, for instance, had told Hardy that he was collecting money to give him a comfortable nest-egg. He already had £100 and would collect more shortly from his rich friends. But after much tiresome prevaricating, a mere £40 was all that eventually came to Hardy from this source.

Hardy had similar frustrations when he tried to recover the mass of material which had been impounded at the time of his arrest. Besides the LCS records, there were personal documents including two Bills of Exchange worth about £200. He wrote to several Ministers but none even favoured him with a reply. He finally petitioned the King but this too was ignored. Hardy saw no alternative but to resign himself to the loss.

But if his noble patrons deserted him and his powerful enemies ignored him, Hardy's real friends never forgot him. For them Guy Fawkes Day – 5 November – became more important as a celebration of Hardy's acquittal, and they instituted a commemoration dinner which, remarkably, was held annually for the next fifty years or so. While he was still active, Hardy attended as guest of honour and main speaker. A writer in *The Times*, on the occasion of Hardy's funeral, recorded that 'he would modestly and briefly return his acknowledgement [of the toasts] always, however, telling some new anecdote'. Four of his responses are printed in an appendix to his *Memoir*: they each run to five or six pages, modest but hardly brief.

The most interesting revelation Hardy made in these addresses is that when he originally formed the LCS he had hoped and expected that, from among the men who in the early 1780s had written those seminal pamphlets which had opened his eyes, there would be 'men of talents who had time to devote for promoting the cause [and who] would step forward', so that 'we, who were the framers of it, who had neither time to spare from our daily employments, nor talents for conducting so important an undertaking, would draw into the background'. But none did step forward: what had happened? They were not all dead, he supposed, nor surely had they 'altogether relinquished' their former convictions. Hardy's conclusion was that this was not as a result of negligent desertion. His diagnosis was 'that an alarm was created among that class by the uncommon appearance of the popular Societies and their active exertions in diffusing political knowledge among their brethren' – and he was probably right. Cartwright had retreated to his country estates and became active again in the reform movement only after the 'popular' societies had been finally suppressed; Horne Tooke, for all his occasional helpfulness, had never believed in universal suffrage; and even the Duke of Richmond lost his enthusiasm for it.

It was left to the 'tradesmen, shopkeepers and mechanicks' to discover and develop their own talents. And they did this with remarkable effect, to which the government's heavy measures against them bear witness. Equally striking were the effects on the members themselves. 'It induced men to read books', wrote Place in his *Autobiography*, 'instead of wasting their time in public houses, it taught them to respect themselves, and to desire to educate their children. The discussions in the divisions, in the Sunday evening readings, and in small debating meetings, opened to them views which they had never before taken. They were compelled by these discussions to find reasons for their opinions, and to tolerate others.' Place attended the first anniversary dinner in 1795 but not again until 1822. He was then gratified to find himself recognised by no less than twenty-four men, most of whom he had not set eyes upon in the intervening twenty-seven years. As members of the LCS they had been journeymen or shopmen, but 'they were now all in business', Place writes, 'all flourishing men. Some were rich most of them had families to whom they had given or were giving good educations. The society had been to a very considerable extent, and in some cases the whole means of inducing them to desire to acquire knowledge the consequence of which was their bringing up a race of men and women as superior in all respects to what they otherwise would have been.' And Place went on to reflect that 'if twenty-four such men were found in one room at one time, how many such men must there be in the whole country ... Every person with whom I have conversed has acknowledged the benefit he derived, and the knowledge he obtained from having been a member of the society.'

On the night of 16 October 1797 there was a less happy demonstration by Hardy's friends of their concern for his well being. The occasion was the celebration in London of a British naval victory over the Dutch. As Hardy's house was an obvious target for the drunken crowds who ranged the streets, his friends had anticipated trouble. And, according to John Binns:

> Hardy would not allow his windows to be illuminated, and they were not only threatened to be broken, but the more violent royalists declared they would sack his house. These threatenings were noised abroad, and about 100 men, chiefly members of the society, many of them Irish, armed with good shillelaghs, took post early in the evening in front of, and close to, the front of Hardy's house. As night approached an immense crowd gathered in the street; many and violent were the attacks and efforts to get possession of the house, and many were the wounds inflicted by fists and sticks. There were no firearms used nor stones thrown, except at the windows. About 11 o'clock at night, a troop of horses were sent to keep the peace, and soon after the crowd dispersed. I was never in so long-continued and well-conducted a fight as was that night made by those who defended Hardy's house against such overwhelming numbers.

There are of course other contemporary accounts of this bloody night, which differ somewhat from Binns' boyish exultations; but whatever the truth of the matter, it is clear that though Hardy had enemies he was never without friends, and day to day his life was peaceful. The LCS continued its work, but Hardy took virtually no active part in it. He never publicly explained the reasons for this but possibilities readily suggest themselves: the trauma of the trial, the cruel vilifications and derisive sneers printed in sections of the press, his narrow escape from a public hanging; in addition, he probably knew that a vindictive government, smarting from its defeats in court, would have been only too eager to seize him again if he gave them the least cause (and on a lesser charge than treason they could hope for a heavy prison sentence, perhaps even transportation).

On the other hand, when he was released he had found himself a national hero, and this might have persuaded him to resume his leadership. But he was not that kind of a man, he was not a power-seeker. His spur to action had always come from inner conviction. So it is to his inner feelings that we need to look: his first action on regaining his liberty was to escape from the adulation of the crowds to seek his wife's grave. This was surely the most hurtful trauma that he had suffered: not the threat to his own life but the death of his former gentle companion.

As to the other two who had stood trial with Hardy, Tooke returned to writing his *Diversions from Purley*, resuming his philological studies.[1] Towards the end of 1796 he stood for election to one of the Westminster parliamentary seats. He was not successful. Four years later he was returned for the very rotten borough of Old Sarum only to find himself disqualified as a former minister of the Church. He spent his remaining years at his home in Wimbledon, where he died in 1812. Thelwall appears to have lain low for only a year after his acquittal. Then he returned to the LCS to join their campaign against the outrageous 'Two Acts' – a story to be followed in the next section.

41

The fear of insurrection continued to haunt the government following its defeat at the Old Bailey: anti-war feeling was growing, the armies in Europe were suffering humiliating defeats, there was a severe food shortage – despite a relatively good harvest, much of it had to be exported to feed the armies – bread riots were widespread. (The price of wheat, which had hovered around 50 shillings a quarter for many years, jumped to 75s in 1795 and 78s in 1796.) And as 1795 advanced they were getting reports that the LCS was reviving.

The government spies who had been unmasked at the trials could no longer be used, but there was still one spy operating successfully. This was James Powell, who had worked his way onto the executive committee of the LCS, and indeed is found to be signing letters as President in January 1795. One of these, addressed to the Duke of Portland, the new Minister for Home Affairs , invited the government to send official observers, rather than spies, to the LCS committee meetings.

This notice of the Society's law-abiding intentions may have been due to the influence of Francis Place who had joined the LCS in June 1794 and whose organisational skills and political acumen were quickly recognised. He soon gained a seat on the committee and in fact chaired it for many months in 1795, directing its affairs with great efficiency at a time when the rapid expansion of the Society threatened to over-whelm it with an unmanageable load of business. The LCS Minutes record that in July of that year there were 23 Divisions with 485 attend-ing; and by September this had expanded to 64 Divisions with 1760 attending. Place puts the total membership at this time at 2000. (Membership of course would be higher than the number attending on any particular occasion.) So this was a period of the most rapid growth ever of the Society; and provincial societies were also reviving. In the twelve months from September 1795, the LCS Minutes record corre-spondence with no less than twenty different groups from Dundee to Truro.

The committee resolved to take on something of the function of the now defunct SCI: to educate 'that part of our Countrymen who are ignorant of the true source of their sufferings by means of cheap publi-cations which would propagate the need for a reform of parliament'. They were also faced with two perennial preoccupations – trying to rescue the Society from the burden of debt, and trying to reach agree-ment on a revised constitution. It was hoped that sale of their publications would help with the former. As to the latter, the view from the committee room was seemingly irreconcilable with that of the Divisions who were suspicious of being dictated to by their leaders. This is not surprising, given the democratic orientation of the member-ship. But the debates led to much bitterness and eventually (30 March) to the secession of Division 12 which declared 'you have assumed power which never belonged to you; you have treated our Delegate with contempt and reproach; you have despised and neglected our motions...' They formed a breakaway society which they called the London Reforming Society. And a week later Division 16 addressed a lengthy letter of complaint to the committee and announced their intention to go independent with yet another new society to be called the Friends of Liberty.

These events certainly threatened the integrity of the LCS, and Powell's reports must have raised hopes in government circles that the thing was about to disintegrate. But Place's hand is again evident in the committee's resolve to refrain from recrimination and to set about building positive relationships with the new societies, reaching an agreement, for instance, to co-operate in the production of pamphlets.

In June the committee decided it was time to make themselves felt by holding a public General Meeting. It was a bold move, defiant of the government who might be supposed to be looking for some pretext for action to reverse the defeats at the trials still only six months distant. The agenda of this meeting followed a familiar pattern: two Addresses were read, one to the Nation and one to the King, calling for a 'free and equal Representation', the dismissal of his ministers 'who have so long insulted us and betrayed our dearest interests', and an end to the ravages of 'a cruel and destructive War'. But there were difficulties in getting the *Address to the King* into the royal hands, and after fruitless hours of waiting in the office of the Secretary of State the committee decided to abandon the pursuit. Instead they planned a further General Meeting at which they would present a *Remonstrance to the King* for his failure to respond to their first Address. This second meeting was held on 26 October in a field adjacent to Copenhagen House and again drew a very large crowd ('upwards of Two Hundred Thousand Citizens,' the organisers claimed.)

Whether this 'remonstrance' ever reached the King is doubtful. But it happened that, only three days after the LCS meeting, His Majesty, on his way from St James's Palace to open Parliament, was met by a very large and very hostile crowd shouting its protests against the war and against the shortage of bread. Accounts of what happened next vary: we do not know whether a single missile or several were hurled at the King's coach, or whether the missiles were stones or bullets. One at least, probably a stone, broke a window of the carriage. Similarly, on his return journey, was it that a man was simply pushed against the

King's coach, or did he open the door and attempt to drag His Majesty out? At any rate the Life Guards galloped up to escort the royal person to Buckingham House to enjoy his dinner.

The government preferred the more sensational of these stories and represented the incident as an attempt on the life of the monarch. A Proclamation by the King appeared in the papers on 5 November, the very day when members of the LCS were preparing to celebrate the first anniversary of Hardy's acquittal. This proclamation opened with the words:

> Whereas it hath been represented to us, that, immediately before the opening of the present Session of Parliament, a great number of persons were collected in fields in the neighbourhood of the Metropolis, by Advertisements and Hand-bills, and that divers inflammatory discourses were delivered, and divers proceedings were had, tending to create groundless jealousy and discontent, and to endanger the public peace, and the quiet and safety of our faithful subjects: And whereas it hath also been represented to us, that divers seditious and treasonable papers have been lately distributed, tending to excite evil disposed persons to acts endangering our Royal Person ...

The reference of course was to the meeting of the LCS at Copenhagen House and to their published Addresses. Pitt had persuaded His Majesty (and perhaps himself too) that it was this LCS meeting which had incited the people to the 'attack' on his Royal Person. Thus represented, it was the ideal occasion to introduce into parliament two bills which had doubtless been already prepared, awaiting a suitable moment for unveiling. The first, *An Act for the Safety and Preservation of His Majesty's Person against Treasonable and Seditious Practices and Attempts*, was presented to the House of Lords by Lord Grenville. Essentially this extended the definition of treason and sedition to include inciting people to hatred or contempt of the Sovereign or the Government. Then on November 10th, Pitt invited the Commons to approve the second of these two Bills, an *Act to prevent Seditious Meetings and Assemblies* which was to ban meetings of more than fifty persons called to promote constitutional changes. A magistrate would be able to order such a meeting to disperse and the death penalty would await any who ignored his order.

These measures became known as the 'Two Acts': they were accompanied by a fierce campaign of intimidation against those who, with equal fervour, lamented what they saw as the death of liberty. The opposition in the Commons had been weakened by a split amongst the Whigs, many of whom had joined the government. But the remainder, the Foxite Whigs as they were called, argued strongly, in the Chamber and outside. against these repressive Bills. The liberal press took up the chorus, the *Morning Chronicle* (13 November 1795) declaring them to be:

> ... a complete surrender of the liberty of the press, and of the gift of speech are necessary to the due obedience of these laws ... We call upon any honest lawyer to say, whether His Majesty could give his Royal assent to these bills, in their present shape, without a violation of the sacred oath he took to preserve to the people of England the great fundamental principles of their liberty.

And even *The Times* (16 November 1795) had qualms:

> We approve with some exceptions the general principle of the Bill but we differ most widely as to the time of its proposed duration... We for our parts would wish the Bill to be FOR ONE YEAR ONLY ... there would be no difficulty in renewing it. To make the duration of the Bill the period of the life of the present Sovereign appears to us impolitic, and liable to create an unnecessary ferment in the nation.

Meetings and petitions were reported from all over the country – in Launceston and Leicester, in Glasgow, Cambridge, Stowmarket and Edinburgh, in Newport and Dundee, in Reading and Yarmouth and Warwick ... and in numerous London districts. The Corresponding Society naturally joined, or led, these protests. Two general meetings were organised. The first, on 12 November attracted an enormous crowd – 'probably the largest ever assembled', according to Place. Addresses to the King, the Lords and the Commons were read and approved; there were speeches from John Gale Jones and from Thelwall (who had now rejoined the Society). Following this meeting the Society opened a petition against the Two Acts.

A handbill was issued on 23 November in response to the numerous attacks that were being made against the Society. This was *An Explicit Declaration of the Principles and Views of the London Corresponding Society*: Place records that at the time it was thought to be a masterpiece, though he himself concedes only that was 'very creditable... a manly spirited production remarkable well calculated for the time.' Extracts from this handbill are reproduced on p146.

At their second meeting the LCS invited two non-members as main speakers – Matthew Browne, the editor of the Sheffield periodical *The Patriot*, and William Frend. Many members of parliament joined the large crowd, including the Whig leader Fox, for this was an occasion of general protest rather than for the transaction of LCS business. The protests continued right up to the last moment. But Pitt's majority was secure and the two bills were passed through parliament and became a part of the law of the land on 18 December.

The re-emergence of Thelwall into LCS activity appears to have been stimulated by his outrage at the Two Acts. He resumed his political lectures though when the Acts became law he was obliged to keep his audiences to under fifty and he took the added precaution of billing the subject of his lectures as Roman History! This gave him immunity from prosecution but not from other unpleasant attentions which, if not actually instigated by the government, appear to have had their blessing. In the summer of 1796 Thelwall embarked on a lecture-tour of East Anglia. At Great Yarmouth one of his meetings was invaded by a party of sailors (organised by officers on board a naval sloop anchored in the harbour) who laid about the audience with bludgeons and attempted to abduct Thelwall himself, apparently with a view to impressing him into naval service. He brandished his pistol at his attackers and with the help of friends he escaped. Bravely, Thelwall resumed his lectures the following night and apparently did not lack an audience even though the sailors had smashed all the chairs. Other groups of riotous seamen accompanied by press-gangs attacked his meetings first at Kings Lynn and again at Wisbech. The audiences were ready to defend him and to guard their right to hear him and the attackers were repulsed. On other occasions in Derby, Stockport and Norwich he had to defend himself with his pistol, while at Ashby-de-la-Zouch he was pursued fifteen miles to Mountsorrel where he was rescued by a courageous constable. Elsewhere, magistrates had refused protection.

By the summer of '97 Thelwall had had enough of this dangerous harassment. Leaving his family in Derby, he headed for the West Country where he hoped to find a little peace. In fact he found Coleridge and Wordsworth and stayed a few months with them. But these poets themselves had something of a Jacobin reputation – not as lurid as Thelwall's but colourful enough to cause alarm in the neighbourhood and to attract the attention of a government spy – in fact, the one-time Bow Street runner Walsh who had arrested Thelwall for trea

---

The Principles of the London Corresponding Society

I. This Society is, and ever has been, firmly attached to the principles of Equality ... Social equality appears to them to consist in the following things: 1. The acknowledgement of equal rights. 2. The existence of equal laws for the security of those rights. 3. Equal and actual representation, by which ... the invasion of those laws can be prevented ... In their ideas of equality, they have never included (nor, till the associations of alarmists broached the frantic notion, could they ever have conceived that so wild and detestable a sentiment could have entered the brain of man) as the equalisation of property ...

II. With respect to particular forms and modifications of Government, this Society conceives ... that the disputes and contentions about these ... are marks only of weak and inconsiderate minds ... Their attention has been uniformly addressed to more essential objects – to the peace – the social order – and the happiness of mankind; and these ... might be sufficiently secured by the *genuine spirit* of the British Constitution. They have laboured therefore ... not to overthrow, but to *restore* and *realize* that Constitution ... Peaceful reform, and not tumultuary revolt, is their object ...

III. This Society has always cherished ... the most decided abhorrence of all tumult and violence ... At the same time they do not wish to be understood as giving ... any sort of countenance to the *detestable and delusive doctrines of Passive Obedience and Non-resistance.* This is a system which none but *hypocrites* will *profess*, and none but *slaves* will *practice* ...To resist oppression (when no other means are left) even with the same arms with which it is enforced, is, they are aware, not only a natural right, but a constitutional duty ... But resistance of oppression and promotion of tumult, are, in their minds, distinct propositions ... They trust that the Nation at large is equally sensible of the distinction; and that if the dire necessity ever should arise, when the liberties of Britain must be asserted, not by the voice and the pen, but by the sword, Britons will rally round the standard of Liberty, not like a band of depredators and assassins, but like a Spartan Phalanx: prepared and resolved to a man rather to die at their posts, than to abandon their principles, and betray the Liberties of the country!!!

J. Ashley, Secretary

The above is extracted from an LCS handbill, 23 November 1795, To the Parliament and People of Great Britain. An explicit declaration of the Principles and Views of the London Corresponding Society.

son two years earlier. He must have been excited to be able to report finding this notorious Jacobin joining the other two. As far as Thelwall was concerned, Walsh's prying was as nothing compared to the attacks from sailors and dragoons in East Anglia. But when he tried to find a cottage for himself and his family the alarm in the neighbourhood was such that no-one would consider him as a tenant. Sadly he left Somerset and made his way to Wales, where he did find a home with a smallholding which he worked for a year or two. It was the beginning of his retirement from political life. He subsequently made a living for himself and quite a different kind of reputation, as a teacher of elocution and as a writer.

42

The LCS was obliged to adjust its structure to avoid gatherings of more than fifty people. They did this by introducing a third tier – the Districts – of which there were to be four and to which the Divisions (now limited to 46 members) sent deputies. The Districts in turn sent deputies – one for every five Divisions – to form the General Committee. This done they embarked on a new form of activity aimed at stimulating the growth of allied societies in different parts of the country. Early in 1796 they began to send out deputies ('missionaries') to advise and encourage these less experienced groups. For a start, John Binns was sent to Portsmouth and John Gale Jones to towns in Kent – Rochester, Gravesend, Maidstone.

Naturally the government was well aware of this departure – Powell was still keeping the Ministry well informed – and appears to have watched the deputies carefully. Binns' mission was very soon aborted when 'reliable information' came that he was about to be impressed and sent aboard one of the ships in the harbour. Nevertheless, the committee was encouraged by letters of appreciation from both Portsmouth and Rochester where the reception given to Jones bordered on veneration. So it was decided to send the two off on another mission – this time to Birmingham, a dangerous city for radicals, a city where, according to Binns, 'leaders of the 1790-91 Church and King riots still swaggered' and where magistrates were already alerted to the activities of the local Society.

The news of the arrival of the two deputies from London spread quickly and so many flocked to hear them that neither Jones nor Binns, holding separate meetings, could limit the numbers to the prescribed fifty. Magistrates and constables arrived at Jones's meeting and arrested him in mid-speech. Binns was allowed to finish his meeting but was arrested a few days later, apparently on instructions from London. After interrogation both were bailed, and neither was put on trial till the following year. In fact, legal advisers had warned the government of the likely difficulty of obtaining convictions, but they may have calculated that the effect of the delayed action would be to ensure that the threat of convictions hung over the head of the LCS. If so, the tactic worked: the committee decided to risk no further missionary activity of this kind. Eventually the trials went ahead: Jones was found guilty but was never sentenced, and Binns, charged with uttering seditious words, was acquitted.

The Society was still struggling with its debts. Membership had declined again following the Two Acts. The General Meetings of 1795 had been an additional expense and they now had to meet the costs of the trials of Jones and Binns. In the spring of 1796, partly in the hope of earning some money – but also to propagate their ideas – the committee decided to start the publication of a monthly magazine to be called *The Moral and Political Magazine of the London Corresponding Society*. Place was scathing. 'Another absurdity', he called it. 'A better contrivance to prevent the society paying its debts could hardly have been devised.' He and Ashley tried to dissuade the committee from this venture, and when they failed – the first issue appeared in July 1796 – they resigned their posts as Assistant Secretary and Secretary respectively. As it turned out they were right. The magazine made money with its first issue, but thereafter cost the Society more and more. The Committee was forced to admit its failure and the May '97 issue was the last.

But they remained either incompetent or blithely profligate. By now debts were running at about £200, and some of the money which had been raised for Jones and Binns had to be used for the society's running expenses. Even so, the committee decided to incur the expense of yet another General Meeting. This was the last straw for Place and Ashley. Both men resigned from the committee, and soon after from the Society itself. It is likely that it was not only the management of the finances that they were worried about. The public meeting was a dangerous undertaking, likely to run foul of at least one of the Two

Acts, and Place was not the kind of man willingly to put his head into that kind of noose.

By two o'clock on 31 July several thousands had assembled in a field at St Pancras together with magistrates, constables and soldiers – the LCS estimated that there were two thousand of each of the latter two, with a further six to eight thousand soldiers nearby. Only twenty minutes after the meeting had started, the magistrates called a halt, and six of the leaders were arrested – the LCS president, Hodgson, together with Galloway, Barrow, Stuckey, Benjamin Binns and Ferguson. The crowd was given one hour to disperse.

The six men were examined at Bow Street for several hours and then released on bail to appear at Quarter Sessions. But in fact no proceedings were ever taken against them: it was decided that the charge of seditious words could not be sustained, and this meant that the only charge that could have been brought would have been the difficult one of conspiracy to hold an illegal meeting for seditious purposes. Erskine would surely have found no difficulty in demolishing such a charge.

But the incident was disturbing for many in the LCS leadership. Place and Ashley were not the only ones to be perturbed by the committee's provocative daring. Three days after the meeting, a letter in which twenty members announced their withdrawal from the Society was sent to the committee. 'We deplore the increase of factious spirit', they wrote, 'the preference given to measures most inconsiderate and violent.'

There were probably more than twenty members uneasy at the signs of growing militancy among the leadership,which was strikingly manifested in what turned out to be the Society's last publication – *An Address to Irish Nation*, issued on 30 January 1798. The language was not gentle. As Englishmen (though the writer, John Binns, was Irish and a member of the organisation United Irishmen), they expressed regret for 'the enormous cruelties ... practised in every Corner of Ireland', and asked 'Why has all this Inhumanity, this savage Barbarity been committed?' According to the *Address*, the reason given by the government was that 'some Men formed societies calling themselves UNITED IRISHMEN who swore in the most solemn manner to persevere in endeavouring to form a Brotherhood of affection among Irishmen of every religion and persuasion for the purpose of effecting Reforms which we do not think expedient."

'If this is a crime,' the LCS Address declared, 'then we too plead guilty ... As our fellow Men in Ireland live under the same FORM of

Government and are in fact governed by the same Men [as us] we enter-tain the well-grounded Fear that what HAS been done in Ireland MAY be done in Britain.' They concluded: 'May your Governors ... learn that Governments are made for the People and not People for Governments ... that just Revenge of a People is ever proportional to the Injuries that they have received; that the Injured cannot always be repressed; that Forbearance beyond a certain point becomes Cowardice.'

Place described this document as rodomontade. It was certainly not diplomatic, published at a time when the government were anxiously expecting an invasion by the French and believed that the United Irishmen were likely to assist in it and were perhaps in secret contact in the planning of it. This was not without reason – an Irish rebellion erupted four months after the publication of this Address and a French invasion, though speedily and brutally crushed, followed in August.

In mid-April 1798 a deposition was taken from the government spy Powell, recorded anonymously as 'Informant'. He remarks that owing to the arrests following the aborted General Meeting the LCS commit-tee had not met so frequently' but they do still meet and that particularly last Tuesday [April 10?] they debated as to the possibility of getting Arms to be in readiness & co-operate with the French upon their intended Invasion of England. Informant was not present but understood that such was the subject... Informant further says that there now exists & has for these twelve months existed a Society calld the United Englishmen [the object of which] is to form a republic thro' the Means of the French.' Powell went on to describe the organisation, activities, meeting place, etc of this society in which he himself had enrolled and had been made a Captain of one of its seven sections! Evans and Galloway were also members and, with the two Binns as 'principal Members' of the United Irishmen, communication with the LCS was 'constant'. Two members of the LCS (Dr Watson and John Bone) had been sent to get in touch with the naval mutineers at Portsmouth and the Nore.

Although perhaps exaggerated, this account was certainly based on fact. Place was aware of these revolutionary plans – 'a more ridiculous project was never entered by the imaginations of men out of Bedlam'. At one point he had intended to send for Evans, Benjamin Binns and 'a foolish fellow, their coadjutor named James Powell', to tell them that he and others would apprise Mr Ford (the very man, a magistrate at the Treasury, who had taken Powell's deposition!) as to what they were about. Place was dissuaded from doing so by the others, including

Colonel Despard (later to be executed for his part in the alleged Cato Street conspiracy), who thought this would be dishonourable.

The government, however, did not think Powell such a foolish fellow. They arrested thirteen men on 18 April as Evans was trying to organise a division of United Englishmen, and on the following day a meeting of the general committee of the LCS was interrupted by Bow Street officers who arrested all but one of them. The one who 'escaped' was, unsurprisingly, James Powell.[2] In the next few days there were more arrests – Benjamin Binns, John Bone, Thomas Spence, Galloway and Col. Despard were all taken in: some were held only for a few weeks but others, habeas corpus having been suspended again in April, were not freed till much later, the last in 1801.

This spate of arrests effectively spelled the end of the London Corresponding Society. It might have recovered, but in the following year, on 12 July, it was outlawed, along with the Societies of the United Englishmen and the United Irishmen.

43

Approaching sixty, Cartwright found the management of his Lincolnshire estate more of a chore than it had ever been. He tried to entice his nephew Edmund to take it over but the young man held a commission in the militia and his uncle had to agree that it would not be right for him to quit 'before the end of the war' (still twenty years away, though of course they were not to know this). So there was no escape. His appetite for political activity, re-kindled by the heady weeks at the trials in London, had to remain unsatisfied at least for the time being.

Not that he would have found much support. Tooke wrote to him in 1797, 'I think the cause of reform is dead and buried.' Cartwright pencilled in the margin of this letter 'But J.C. believes in the resurrection'. Perhaps so, but there was little evidence in favour of such faith. His old reformist associates had all retreated into frightened silence. The SCI had disappeared. Even the Duke of Richmond had lost his zeal and had taken a government post. Fox had never been a reliable ally of reform; the Whigs no longer mentioned the subject and when the government arrested entire LCS committee the Opposition raised no objection.

Since the Habeas Corpus Act had been suspended once more, political prisoners could be left to idle in their cells, without trial, and with no help to be expected from their one-time middle-class allies. 'I never could have believed that he would leave us in the lurch,' one of the prisoners was reported in *The Times* as saying on reading Sheridan's speech in the Commons. But they were not deserted by their real friends. Francis Place energetically organised a fund to be collected for the support of their families. He was helped in this by William Frend, and he enlisted Hardy as treasurer. Together they continued this work for several years until the last prisoner was released.

Cartwright of course had never appeared to be much of an ally for the LCS until perhaps he sat through Hardy's trial. There is no telling what his reaction to the outlawing of the LCS and of their militant associates the United Irishmen and the United Englishmen might have been had he been in circulation at the time. It is quite likely that he would have regarded the removal of this raggle-taggle as no great loss to the cause of parliamentary reform: this was an issue to be settled by the educated classes. On the other hand, his sympathies were with the Irish who, as he saw it, were rebelling against the same intolerant denial of rights with which Pitt, with the backing of a corrupt parliament, was threatening the British nation.

This comes to light in a letter that he wrote in 1798 to his nephew who was faced with the question as to whether he should volunteer for service in Ireland with his militia regiment. He asked Edmund whether he knew enough about the recent history of the Irish to decide 'whether or not the resistance of the people be justifiable or the contrary?' And if he did not, he would be leaving it to chance 'whether the acts you commit are to be justifiable homicide or murder.' To support such action 'under the present ministry ... were to unsheath the sword to establish a hideous despotism over both islands ... If Ireland be once reduced to slavery by English armies, Irish armies will be made to return the favour, and to subjugate the people of England.' All this was not far from the ideas that the LCS were propagating (See p149-50) but to Edmund it probably seemed no more than the familiar ravings of his dear old eccentric uncle: he ignored the arguments and joined his regiment in Ireland.

In 1805 Cartwright found a tenant for his estate and took his wife and niece to live in Enfield. He was now approaching seventy, but his thoughts were not for an easeful retirement. He was intent on resuming his enduring interest, the quest for parliamentary reform. The political scene had changed somewhat since he was last engaged in this work. In 1804 Pitt had been reinstated in office after a three-year break, and had proceeded to organise an alliance with Austria, Russia and Sweden to restrain Napoleon's conquering armies. Nelson's victory at Trafalgar had put paid to French sea-power, finally removing the threat of invasion. But this was about the only success that the allies had chalked up. Napoleon, having added the crown of Italy to his Imperial title, had turned his attention to sweeping the Austrian armies out of Germany. His triumph there had been completed with his victory at Austerlitz, a blow to the allies which is reputed to have killed Pitt – though a surfeit of port may well have helped.

Cartwright would have shed few tears at the passing of this man of 'direful power'. He might even have looked hopefully at the succeeding administration – the so-called 'Ministry of all talents', chiefly Whigs headed by Lord Grenville, with Fox as Foreign Secretary. But he judged politicians mainly on their attitudes to parliamentary reform and there was little likelihood of any advance of that cause from either Grenville or Fox. In the event Fox died after only nine months in office, and Charles Grey took over the leadership of the Whigs. Grey was eventually to pilot the first great Reform Bill through parliament – but only after another twenty-five years of agitation.

Cartwright contributed to that agitation but did not live to see the culmination, such as it was, of his life's main ambition. But he continued his struggle with extraordinary energy for a man of his age and failing health. He was forced to acknowledge that there was little to be hoped for from the Whigs – he resigned from the Whig Club in 1806 – and looked instead to the Radicals, now led by Sir Francis Burdett. Even here support was uncertain. Burdett himself, though presenting a reformist front, became increasingly equivocal – rejecting, for instance, the idea of universal suffrage. Cartwright seems to have decided that the future lay in extra-parliamentary activity. It is true that he accepted an invitation to stand as a candidate for Boston in 1806, but he did not expect to be elected. In fact in his election addresses he told the voters that they might well find men with 'more strength, more learning, more knowledge and more talent, than myself.' Instead of pressing his case, he used the election as an occasion to preach sermons on the duties of the electorate – which should not include seeking bribes from the candidates. 'A vote is not in the nature of a chattel,' he wrote, 'that we can legally or morally sell, or give away, for any private gain ...[it] is a sacred right held in trust, to be exercised only for the good of the country.' He was not elected.

His three election addresses were later published in Cobbett's *Political Register*. Cobbett was one of Cartwright's new allies, a largely self-educated man whose father ran a tavern in Farnham. He had served in the army in America and soon after his return to England in 1800 he started publishing his *Register*, an influential periodical that ran for the next thirty years or so. It began with none of the radical ideas that were to become its stock-in-trade. Still influenced by his army experience, Cobbett was at first keen to support the Tory government in its war with France. However, within a few years Cobbett was turning his attention more to his own origins, to the hardships of the peasantry deprived of their common lands by the enclosures policy, and he became convinced that, because of the antiquated procedures of election, parliament was no longer working for the good of the people. So the columns of the *Register* began to be filled with calls for parliamentary reform, inveighing against the rotten boroughs, the bribery and corruption that infested the political body.

Although he was not of the class that Cartwright had usually hobnobbed with, Cobbett was an obvious ally at a time when the Major met with nothing but dismissive apathy. It is true that two motions for reform were introduced into the Commons at about this time. The first came from Burdett in 1809 but it attracted only fifteen votes in its favour; a year later Thomas Brand found much more support though not enough to get anywhere near the statute book. But both these motions were for very mild reforms and moved Cartwright to publish a pamphlet (*The Comparison* ...) contrasting what he called 'mock reform' or 'half reform' with his full notion of constitutional reform.

In 1810 Cartwright again moved his household, this time into central London, Buckingham Gate, 'to be nearer my work'. Burdett also moved, or rather was moved, into the Tower of London, as a result of his defence of one John Gale Jones. Formerly a prominent member of the Corresponding Society, and now secretary to a debating society, Gale Jones had published a motion vehemently questioning the Commons' practice of excluding 'strangers' from its debates. His motion was considered a breach of privilege and he was arrested. Burdett bravely questioned the right of the Commons to do this and, for this affront to parliamentary power, was himself arrested – ironically, when the sergeant-at-arms, with military backing, arrived to arrest him, he was peacefully instructing his young son in the provisions of the Magna Carta!

Burdett received much public support, at least in his own constituency of Westminster, and Cartwright joined with Cobbett and Francis Place in successfully agitating for his release. Place was another unusual associate of Cartwright's at this period, but one with an ambivalent attitude to the old campaigner – he admired his perseverance but scorned his political naivety.

Back in the centre of things, Cartwright now tried to gather together the disparate factions for reform. To Wyvill he wrote: 'Let us cooperate: let us reason together ... let us harmoniously yield each to the other, as far as possible, without a desertion of principle.' Cartwright was not perhaps the ideal person for such an enterprise: he had held tenaciously to his own principles over the last fifty years, scarcely having yielded a point, and was still ready to deride those faint-hearted advocates of 'mock reform'. But perhaps now, as he entered his seventies, he was ready to be more accommodating; indeed a few years later he even allowed himself to modify his demand for universal suffrage to one for a taxpayer franchise.

He set up two 'reform dinners', one at the Crown and Anchor and a second one in Hackney. There were many, notably the Whig parliamentarians, who refused Cartwright's invitations, and the speeches of those who did attend dwelt more upon differences than possible agreements. But there was one constructive outcome – the formation in 1812 of what was called the Hampden Club (named after the Civil War hero). The founding members of the Club stated its object to be 'securing to the people the free election of their Representatives in the Commons House of Parliament'. The 'people' were defined by implication in another resolution which insisted that taxation and representation were inseparable. Like the SCI of old, the Club was intended for the more affluent, demanding as a membership qualification an income of at least £300 p.a. and requiring an annual subscription of £2. But in fact it became the inspiration for quite a large number of workers' Hampden Clubs, formed a few years later by groups up and down the country.

This development was at least in part stimulated by the 'political tours' which Cartwright now undertook. In 1811 he had been in the Midlands when Luddite protests were raging against unemployment in the textile industry, which was caused by the loss of overseas markets and the new machines being introduced into the textile industry (some of them the invention of Cartwright's brother Edmund). These events had provoked in Cartwright a flurry of conflicting reactions: his compassion was aroused by the dreadful conditions, the near-starvation, being suffered by the workers and their families; but his reverence for private property led him to condemn the Luddite tactic. He was, however, equally opposed to the use of the military in suppressing the workers' violent protests. In a letter to the *Recorder* of Nottingham he told how he was 'shocked whenever I see the law carried into execution by the sword of a standing army, as, on every such occasion, the constitution is stabbed in the vitals ...[it] is complete evidence that a military despotism actually exists' – this was quite a mellowing in attitude from a man who once advised his neighbours in Lincolnshire to face their workers with muskets and bayonets!

Perhaps this was the first time in his life that Cartwright's sympathies had turned towards the distress of working people. Such feelings were reinforced when, in 1812, he set out on the first of his political tours. It took him through Leicester to Manchester where he hoped to attend the trial of thirty-seven men who had been arrested three months earlier at a meeting to consider a petition calling for parliamentary reform. They were charged with having administered 'an unlawful oath', for which the penalty could be transportation. Cartwright arrived a day too late, but was greeted with 'the agreeable news of the acquittal' of the men. From Manchester he went on to Liverpool, Halifax, Sheffield and Nottingham, where he spent his 72nd birthday, holding or attending meetings along the way.[3]

Against the advice of many of his friends, who feared he might get caught up in the growing unrest in the country, Cartwright set off on another tour in the midwinter of the following year. The first part of his journey followed much the same route as before, but from Manchester he went to Birmingham and thence into the west country. It was during this tour that, as he was chatting with a group of mostly 'working mechanics' at an inn in Huddersfield, a party of constables and soldiers interrupted them – 'a very rude interference of civil and military professors of loyalty', in Cartwright's words – with a warrant for Cartwright's arrest. His papers were searched and the next morning he was brought before a magistrate. But since they found nothing in Cartwright's possession more seditious than some draft petitions to parliament the case was dismissed.

It is interesting to find Cartwright in this company of rude mechanicals – a new experience for him. 'I discover in the mass of middle and working class, a very general sense of wrong and misery, and a very general disposition to petition for a reform of that house [of

Commons], the corruption of which was generally supposed to be the cause.' This belief had been the driving force of the LCS, of course, but for Cartwright the case for reform had always been more abstract – the restoration of ancient liberties. Now in his old age he was discovering the more urgent needs for reform and was finding new allies in place of those of his own class who had evaporated.

The peace dividend anticipated at the end of the Napoleonic wars failed to materialise, as peace dividends are prone to do. From 1815 to at least 1820, the lot of working people in Britain deteriorated still further; unrest grew, and with it the intervention of the military and the proliferation of government spies, informers and provocateurs. Undoubtedly there were a number of violent militants among the workers, and from time to time there were angry riots by hungry and desperate mobs. But for the most part the demand for reform was expressed in fairly peaceful meetings, marches and petitions. And it was during this period that Hampden Clubs spawned throughout the industrial North and Midlands. Roughly modelled on the London club, though of course without such high membership fees, the new societies mainly concerned themselves with informing their members by reading from such publications as the *Political Register* or the cheaper version *Twopenny Trash*. Their members were very ready, and perhaps flattered, to welcome Cartwright – now known as 'father of reform' – at their meetings, though this now bald septuagenarian must have seemed more like a grandfather. No doubt the draft petitions found in Cartwright's possession by the Huddersfield magistrate were intended for groups such as these. The savagery of the military facing this growing protest movement culminated in the notorious Peterloo massacre, when sabre-wielding troops charged a large gathering in St Peter's Fields at Manchester. Several were killed and hundreds were injured. Remonstrations were loud and widespread, but the government responded with even more repressive measures – the so-called Six Acts. Though far from popular, these Acts seemed to be vindicated by the uncovering in 1820 of a latter-day Gunpowder Plot, the Cato Street conspiracy to assassinate the entire cabinet as they dined together.

It is very probable that Cartwright would have been at the St Peter's Fields on that bloody Monday in 1819 but for the fact that about this time he was being indicted at Leamington along with half-a-dozen other 'malicious, seditious, evil-minded persons' with 'designing to raise disaffection and discontent in the minds of His

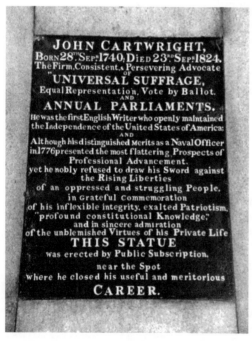

Illustration 6: John Cartwright's memorial statue, Cartwright Gardens, London

Cartwright was in fact born on 17 September by the old calendar, but after the change-over to the new calendar he celebrated his birthday on the 28th – hence the date on the inscription

Majesty's subjects.' This could have landed him in gaol, an uncomfortable prospect for a man of seventy-nine. He negotiated bail and in fact was not brought to trial until August 1820. Along with all the other defendants he was found guilty, but had to wait for almost another year before hearing his sentence. Cartwright was the only one of the accused who escaped imprisonment, perhaps because of his age, or possibly on account of his status and reputation. Instead, he was fined £100 which he paid before leaving court, counting out the gold coins slowly and deliberately from a large canvas bag, and remarking with dry ambiguity, 'I believe they are all *good* sovereigns'.

Cartwright had made a third, and highly successful, tour in 1815 – this one to Scotland, but now in his eighties he at last began to allow himself a more restful life. He did continue his very extensive correspondence, he made occasional journeys to visit old friends and he enjoyed evenings of conversation with his family and with occasional visitors. In 1824 it was evident that his strength was failing. 'My life glides smoothly towards its close', he wrote to one distant friend. And so it did. He died peacefully on 23 September of that year.

His was a life devoted largely to the single cause of parliamentary reform. It is difficult to believe that as he became aware that he was dying he could not but despair at the almost total lack of tangible achievement, but perhaps he was able to preserve a conviction that he had helped to move the country closer to his own obsessional vision. He would not have been wrong, for had he lived another eight years he would have seen it take its first somewhat tentative step in that direction.

Two years after Cartwright's death a subscription was opened for the making and erection of a statue of the old campaigner. This now stands at Cartwright Gardens near St Pancras in London (see illustration 6) .

44

In 1797 Hardy moved his shoemaker's shop from Tavistock Street to better premises in Fleet Street. Although he was no longer an active member of the LCS, he kept in touch with his old friends, many of whom would visit him for an evening's chat, no doubt asking his advice about their current concerns. Thelwall kept up a regular correspondence with him and of course he usually attended the dinners held each year on 5 November to commemorate his acquittal at the treason trials of 1794. These gatherings attracted anything from 20 to 150 people, mostly ex-LCS members, so they gave him the opportunity to meet still more old friends.

Soon after his move to Fleet Street he became a Freeman of the Cordwainers Company and the Liverymen of the Needlemakers Company (which had developed out of the old trade guilds). He evidently made efforts to engage these Companies in the cause of parliamentary reform for he wrote to Major Cartwright for some assistance in preparing a petition to be submitted by the 'Livery of London Common Hall' (a federation of the Livery Companies of that city). Cartwright replied encouragingly at some length, though distancing himself somewhat from the enterprise. He betrayed a degree of mistrust of such plebeian interventions by quite unnecessarily warning Hardy against any revolutionary solutions that they might be tempted to favour.

By 1815 Hardy's business was suffering the effects of the depression into which the country was sinking. He found he was beginning to lose money, largely as a result of bad debts as many of his creditors fell into bankruptcy. The worry was affecting his health and he decided it was time to retire. He had £700 in savings, which was not enough to buy an annuity, but he reckoned that neither he nor his widowed sister (now living with him) were likely to live more than another seven years and, with their modest needs, those £700 would certainly see them through. He closed his shop and they moved into rooms in Pimlico.

However, with the burden of a failing business lifted, his health improved and by 1823 he found himself still strong and active, but with his savings almost exhausted. He was forced to turn to one of his few remaining rich sympathisers for help. He wrote to Sir Francis Burdett explaining his precarious situation, and received an encouraging reply. Sir Francis, 'having great regard for you, as an honest, sensible, ill-treated man', asked Hardy to be more explicit as to his needs, and enclosed £10 to be going on with. The matter was settled within a couple of months: Hardy was to receive £100 p.a., half to come from Sir Francis and the other half from five anonymous friends 'who know and respect your understanding and integrity'. The money was to be placed in the care of William Frend, from whom Hardy was to draw it as he needed it.

It was a generous act on Burdett's part even if, as a very rich man, the £50 would probably have meant little to him. But it meant everything to Hardy, keeping him from destitution. Frend continued to act as banker until 1827 when he handed the job over to Francis Place. By then Hardy was actually overdrawing the account by 20 to 30 pounds a year and it may be that Frend felt the need for someone more capable than he in restraining these inflationary pressures. If so, Place was a good choice.

The agitation for parliamentary reform which marked the immediate post-war years subsided somewhat in the early 1820s, but then built up again until fears of some revolutionary action convinced enough politicians that they had to take some action. The general election in 1830 on the accession of William IV saw the end of Tory dominance, bringing in the Whigs under Lord Grey who formed the new administration committed to reform. A complicated period of negotiation followed which culminated in what became known as the 'great Reform Bill' of 1832 – 'to prevent the necessity for revolution' in Lord Grey's words, though he added that he was absolutely opposed to annual parliaments, universal suffrage and the [secret] ballot.

Cartwright would have remonstrated at this, but Hardy, perhaps deceived by the hype, was elated to see, as he thought, the work he had started forty years previously now coming to fruition. He used the occasion to write to Lafayette, one of the surviving leaders of the first stages of the French Revolution, congratulating him on the 'late glorious Revolution in France, in July last' and recalling the Address which the LCS had sent to the French National Assembly all those years ago. He went on to remark on his own pleasure 'with the Revolution which has taken place in this country, for revolution it is. The King, and his Ministers are now turned Parliamentary Reformers ... guilty of the very same crime ... High Treason' with which he, Hardy, had been charged in 1794.

Lafayette replied politely though in more restrained terms. (The 1830 revolution in Paris had failed to establish the republic that he had hoped for.) But Hardy may be excused his too-sanguine view of the British Reform Bill that was then in process: his letter was written in April 1831, just before Grey had to call another election when his Bill was rejected. The Whigs were returned in greater strength on the cry of 'The Bill, the whole Bill, and nothing but the Bill'. At the second attempt the Bill was passed by the Commons but thrown out by the Lords. After more violent riots in the country, a third Bill was, still with difficulty, passed through all its stages by June 1832.

Perhaps Hardy could now see that the Reform Act was hardly revolutionary. It could claim to bring about a 60 per cent increase in the franchise; but this still meant that only 18 per cent of the adult male population of England had the vote (with the figure being 12 per cent for Scots and a mere 5 per cent for the Irish). Suffrage was property-based, excluding all but a minority of the working-class. The industrial cities of the Midlands and the North were given some representation and many of the rotten boroughs were eliminated though a substantial number, with only a few hundred voters, remained. The secret ballot had to wait another forty years; bribery and treating continued. Parliaments were to continue to be elected for seven-year periods until 1911 when the present five-year term was introduced. Candidates for parliament were required to have property of a rental-value of at least £300 p.a.: elected members drew no salary for their services, so they needed private incomes or work, such as that of some lawyers, that could be interleaved with their parliamentary duties. The net effect was to leave the composition of the Commons largely as it was, predominantly aristocratic, while extending the franchise to the propertied middle-classes.

This was not at all what the men of the old LCS had been working for and very soon their inheritors, the Chartists, were raising their own protests. Thomas Cooper in his autobiography recalls the first Chartist meeting he attended when the speaker attracted wild applause with his peroration: 'Don't be deceived by the middle classes again. You helped them get their votes – you swelled their cry of "The bill, the whole bill, and nothing but the bill!" But where are the fine promises they made you? Gone with the winds! They said when they had gotten their votes, they would help you get yours. But they and the rotten Whigs have never remembered you. Municipal reform has been for their benefit – not yours. All the other reforms the Whigs boast to have effected have been for the benefit of the middle classes – not for yours ...'[4]

Hardy died on 11 October 1832, just four months after the Reform Bill had completed its troubled passage through parliament. Since he had been out of the public eye for nearly forty years it might be supposed that his death would have attracted little notice. On the contrary, most of the papers recorded his passing, and not just the London ones. The *Norwich Mercury* for instance commented, 'The name of Hardy is associated with the attempt against the liberties of the country in 1794 that is familiar to every native of these kingdoms'.

After a brief account of his trial the notice continued, 'Never were verdicts of Not Guilty more acceptable to the nation, who, in the defeat of Pitt, saw the defeat of plans to crush the remaining liberties of the Country. Mr Hardy was one of the best and kindest of men. All who knew him respected him ...' This is typical of the many notices that appeared in the Press: even *The Times*, which had been so dismissive in the past of this 'presumptuous cobbler', now recalled him as 'a man of simple habits and a most humane and benevolent disposition, passing through a long life with the esteem of everyone who knew him'.

His funeral on 18 October, which was also widely reported, offers even more of striking evidence of the remarkable display of the affection with which he was remembered, particularly among the working-people. The following account is taken from the report printed in the *Examiner*:

FUNERAL OF THE LATE THOMAS HARDY

On Thursday the remains of this eminent reformer were conveyed to their resting-place, attended by a very numerous assemblage of persons. About 12 o'clock, a considerable number of gentlemen assembled at Mr Pritchard's (the undertaker) in Drury-lane. Several old and conspicuous reformers were among them, and they proceeded in fourteen mourning coaches to Charing-cross, where a considerable crowd had assembled. Here the foot procession was formed consisting principally of respectable artisans and mechanics who marched six abreast. About half-past one o'clock the hearse and mourning coaches, containing Mr Hardy's private friends, arrived from his residence at Pimlico, with Sir Francis Burdett's private carriage (Sir Francis not being able to attend personally) and another private carriage, and Mr Hunt M.P. in a barouche. The *cortege* then started in the following order:– the hearse flanked on either side by a walking procession, the mourning coaches, private carriages, Union flag, and foot procession.[5] The line of march being through the Strand, Fleet-street, Ludgate-hill, Old Bailey, Newgate-street, St Martins-le-Grand, Aldersgate-street, Old-street, City-road to Bunhill-fields burial-ground where they arrived about three o'clock. The streets were lined and the houses thronged with spectators, all of whom seemed to take a deep interest in the solemn occasion, and many thousands persons accompanied it to Bunhill-fields. Several shops in Fleet-street, Strand and Ludgate-hill were partially, and some entirely, closed, but when the funeral train arrived

Illustration 7: Hardy's headstone

within the precincts of St. Luke's, scarcely a house was to be found which had not paid to the illustrious dead this tribute of respect. A number of flags and banners emblematic of liberty and union, but bordered with crape, were displayed from different houses, or were suspended across the road. After the coffin was lowered into the grave, which is not more than a hundred yards from the road, the funeral service was read in a very impressive manner by the Rev Dr. Rice, rector of St Luke's, who is an active and zealous reformer, much beloved by his parishioners.

At the conclusion of the service Mr THELWALL addressed the immense multitude, which was variously estimated at from 20,000 to 40,000 persons. He spoke,. apparently, under the influence of strong and excited feelings and was listened to throughout with the utmost attention and decorum.

Thelwall was the only surviving member of the trio who had faced their judges in the 1794 treason trials (Horne Tooke having died twenty years previously). In the course of his funeral oration he declared of Hardy, 'Though not standing foremost in point of talent and genius he stood foremost ... in honest principle, and a firm determination to do the utmost in his power to promote the interest of his fellow-men. He was the first sower of that seed of which, I hope, we are about to reap the fruit and public advantage ... He was a man exhibiting a combination of meekness of spirit and a firmness of determination such as is rarely met with.'

So the bones of Thomas Hardy were laid eight feet deep in the soil of London. According to the Bunhill Fields record books his grave was unmarked until, on 6 November 1836, an imposing headstone was raised by 'A.G., J.B. & R.T'(See illustration 7). The date suggests that this was a part of the annual commemoration of Hardy's acquittal – the dinners continued until 1842. The first two initials are probably those of Alexander Galloway and John Binns; the third one I cannot identify. There were originally lengthy inscriptions on the east and west faces, but these have now worn away; however the wording has been preserved in a history of the Bunhills burial ground published in 1902. The inscriptions read as follows:

Public Duty and Private Worth

To the memory of Thomas Hardy, born in March 3rd 1751, and died October 11th 1832, in the 82nd year of his age. He was a plain and upright man, a steady and inflexible patriot, one of three who, in 1792, commenced the formation of the commended *London Corresponding Society*, for the promotion of a radical reform in the Commons House of Parliament; he was appointed Secretary to that Society in the same year, and filled the office with diligence and ability till his arrest in May 1794, on a charge of High Treason, when he was committed to the Tower, separated from his wife and family for six months, subjected to a nine days' trial at the Old Bailey, and triumphantly acquitted by an honest and independent jury on the 5th November 1794, by which event the corrupt and sanguinary ministry of Mr Pitt was defeated, and a brighter era commenced in the political condition of this country.

Thomas Hardy lived to see a great part of his laudable and enlightened objects fulfilled by the passing of *The Reform Bill*, which will ultimately lead to good and happy government. His memory will be cherished by every friend of freedom, piety and moral rectitude. It will be recorded in the history of this great country, that by his excellent conduct through a long life, he demonstrated that the most humble in society, when guided by their *integrity*, and aided by *perseverance* and *judgement*, are sure to add to the happiness, and the advance of liberties, of mankind.

NOTES

1. S. C. Roberts (later to be Master of Pembroke College, Cambridge) records in a little book, *David of Cambridge*, buying a copy of this book of Tooke's at David's bookstall. The copy had evidently been a gift to Hardy, for inside Mr Roberts found a letter to him from Tooke recalling their joint escape from the hangman's noose.

2. It is an indication of Powell's astute acting of the foolish fellow that his duplicity was never suspected by members of the LCS, including as perceptive a man as Francis Place. But then Place always held to his opinions, obstinately believing them to be based on sound logic. 'Powell was honest but silly', he wrote in his *Autobiography* years later, when he tells how he hid him in his apartment after his 'escape' – 'taking good care that no one who came to see me should see him. With the assistance of friends I procured him a passage to Hamburg. I made him a suit of half military cloaths [Place was a tailor] and sent him to Harwich, from which place he and his wife who joined him proceeded to Hambourg.' The government was fully aware of all this, and Powell continued for some years to send them reports on a number of expatriates living in Continental Europe.

3. Cartwright was born on 17 September 1740, when the old Julian calendar was in force. In October 1752 the Gregorian calendar was introduced into Britain and, to the consternation of many people, 11 days were 'lost'. (4 October was followed by 15 October). So the 365 days from John Cartwright's 12th birthday to his 13th took him to 28 September. This became his birthday date thereafter.

4. Thomas Cooper, a self-educated man from Lincolnshire, moved to Leicester in 1840 to become a reporter on the *Leicester Mercury*. It was in this capacity that he attended this meeting which, together with his subsequent discovery of the hardships of the hosiery workers, began his move into Chartism. He became a leading figure in the movement in Leicester and nationally. 'Municipal reform' refers to the 1835 Municipal Corporations Act, which gave the rising factory bosses the part in local government which they wanted.

5. The Union Flag referred to here is the Flag of the National Union of the Working Classes, a forerunner of the Chartist London Working Men's Association (see Thompson, *The Making of the English Working Class*, p 481).

Appendix 1

Brief Biographies of lesser known actors in this story

MEMBERS OF THE LONDON CORRESPONDING SOCIETY

John Ashley (c.1762-1829) Shoemaker. Secretary LCS. 'A serious thinking man of rather imposing appearance ... of undoubted courage ... honest and sincere.' (Place)

Martin Baxter Silversmith. LCS 1792-94, Chairman 1793.

Benjamin Binns Plumber. Eldest son of successful Dublin businessman (iron-mongery), who was drowned when BB was aged 3. 'A man of much meaner understanding than his brother.' (Place)

John Binns (1772-1860) Plumber. Brother of Benjamin. Voracious reader. Member of United Irishmen. Wrote autobiography *Recollections of Life...* (1854) 'A very well-informed man ... but at times volatile as most Irishmen are.' (Place)

John Bone Bookseller. LCS Asst secretary Feb 1796, Secretary Dec.1796. Committed Christian, unhappy with drift to Deism, he led his Division to secession from LCS, forming London Reformation Society. Arrested 1798. After release wrote various tracts and started periodical *The Reasoner* calling for revolution in morals, etc.

Robert Boyd Publican. LCS 1792-? (Founder member).

Thomas Briellat Pumpmaker. LCS 1793-94? Emigrated to America after prison sentence.

Joseph Burks Clerk, bookseller. Employed at East India House but dismissed on account of LCS membership. LCS Secretary 1794. Left in 1795 to join the breakaway 'Friends of Liberty'. Rejoined 1796.

Lord Daer Radically minded peer. LCS 1792- ?.

Edward Despard (1751-1803). Born in Ireland, joined army at 15 yrs, served in American War, rising to rank of colonel. Returned to England in 1790. LCS committee 1796. Joined United Englishmen. Arrested 1798 for his support of Irish rebellion. Re-arrested on release and jailed till 1800. Again arrested for subversion of servicemen. Tried for High Treason. Executed 1803.

Daniel Eaton (c.1751-1814) Stationer, had shop in Hoxton, then in Bishopsgate St. LCS 1793-?. Arrested 1793, acquitted of seditious libel (selling Paine's *The Rights of Man*). Sept 1793 started *Hog's Wash*, a weekly dealing with peace/reform/treatment of poor/religious toleration etc. Arrested Dec 1793 (having referred to King as a tyrannical game-cock). Acquitted again. This cat-and-mouse treatment continued until he fled to America 1797. Returned 1800. Arrested again 1803, and again 1812. Died in poverty.

Thomas Evans Print-colourer/bracemaker. LCS 1795-99. Secretary 1797-8. A militant Spencean, supporter of United Irishmen, favoured training supporters in use of arms. Imprisoned 1798-1801. Co-founded Spencean philanthropists, 1814. Arrested 1817, held for a year without trial. Retired to Manchester.

John Franklow Tailor. LCS 1793-1796?. Assistant secretary 1793. Founded militant Lambeth Loyal Association in 1794. Indicted for high treason in 1794 but was discharged after other acquittals.

Alexander Galloway Machinist. LCS 1794-99. Assistant secretary 1795-6.

Joseph Gerrald (1763-96). Attorney. LCS 1793-4 Delegate to Edinburgh convention. 1794 sentenced 14 years transportation.

William Gow Watchmaker. LCS 1792 – ? (Founder member).

John Gale Jones (1769-1838) LCS 1794-8. Impoverished family. Merchants Taylor's School, became a surgeon. Slight of frame, possibly consumptive. Found guilty of sedition in 1797 but never sentenced. Continued active in 19th century radical politics. 'Tho a sensible citizen, a scholar & a very decent speaker, he is a compleat Egoist.' (Groves, spy)

John Lovett Hairdresser. LCS 1793-94. Chaired Chalk Farm meeting (Apr.1794) Arrested 1794 with others but was the only one not indicted. May have been a government agent. On release he emigrated to New York, 1795.

Maurice Margarot (1745-1815) Wine-merchant. LCS 1792-93. Chairman 92/3. Delegate to Edinburgh Convention. Sentenced 14 years transportation.

John Martin (?-1798) Attorney. LCS 1792-96. Indicted for treason Oct 1794. Released March 1795

Jasper Moore Warehouseman. 1796 on committee. 1798 Arrested with others on committee. Held till 1801. Emigrated to America.

Matthew Moore Tailor. LCS 1793- ?. 1794 indicted for treason but evaded arrest. 1795-6 on committee. '... of a very dangerous cast. He has abilities ... a close reasoner, perfectly cool ... conciliating ... But there is a shrewdness, a subtlety & craft about him.' (Groves, spy)

Francis Place (1771-1854) LCS June 1795-June 1997. President/Asst Secretary LCS. Apprenticed as leather-breeches maker. Set up his own tailor shop (16 Charing Cross). Managed this so successfully that he retired in 1817 and devoted himself to various reform movements (eg. Chartists, Anti-Corn Law League, repeal of Combination Acts, betterment of educational provision and conditions of working-class).

John Richter (? – 1830) Clerk. LCS 1792 – ?. 1973 Elected to committee.

Arrested 1794. Active in radical politics in 19th cent. Worked with Place. 1814 Secretary to Master Manufacturers.

Thomas Spence (1750-1814) LCS 1792-1799 Born in Newcastle, son of a netmaker, strict dissenting & communitarian Christian. Early on Spence developed his view of the importance of communal ownership of the land. He moved to London & opened a bookshop. Started a penny-weekly *Pig's Meat*. Arrested many times. Involved in the militant Lambeth Loyal Association, convinced of need for revolutionary action. After his death his admirers founded the Society of Spencean Philanthropists, which was involved in insurrectionary attempts at the Spa Fields riot (1816) and the Cato Street conspiracy (1820).

Felix Vaughan, Barrister. Nephew of Horne Tooke. LCS 1792- ? Gave legal advice freely to LCS at various times. Junior counsel in defence team for Horne Tooke.

George Walne Tailor. LCS 1792-94?. Founder member. Brother-in-law to Hardy.

Richard Wild Tailor (foreman). 'Led a loose dissolute life [but after joining LCS was] altogether reformed ... abstemious, industrious'. (Place)

John Williams Wine merchant. LCS 1793-95?.

Henry Redhead Yorke (1772-1813) Born in West Indies, spent much of childhood in Continental Europe. In Paris at the time of French Revolution. Joined LCS and Sheffield SCI. He was a fiery orator. A spell in prison caused him to abandon his radical ideas.

MEMBERS OF PROVINCIAL SOCIETIES

Matthew Browne Sheffield. Edited *Patriot*.

John Gales (1761-1841) Sheffield printer/stationer. Unitarian. Started Sheffield Register. Produced first cheap copy of Paine's *The Rights of Man*. Involved in formation of the first artisans' political society (Sheffield Soc. for Constitutional Information). 1792 started *Patriot*, a fortnightly (3 pence). 1794 indicted on conspiracy charges. Fled to Germany, thence to America where he spent the rest of his life.

Thomas Muir (1765-99) Born in Glasgow. To University aged 10, graduated in divinity 1782. Moved to Edinburgh where in 1792 he started National Association of Friends of the People, which had 87 branches by the following January. As vice-president he called Convention. Arrested Aug 1793. Sentenced 14 years transportation.

Thomas Fyshe Palmer (1747-1802) Unitarian minister. Born in Bedfordshire. 1781 took divinity degree at Cambridge. Then, influenced by Priestley, moved to Scotland (1783) to become Unitarian preacher. Became involved in radical reform politics, joined Friends of Liberty at Dundee (1793). Arrested for sedition in August 93. Sentenced 7 years transportation.

Isaac Saint Leading member of Norwich reform society. 1794 Arrested to be examined by Privy Council.

William Skirving (? – 1796) Son of Lanarkshire farmer. Graduated from Univ of Edinburgh. A deeply religious man. He became involved in the reform movement and was secretary of the Scottish Friends of the People. He was a delegate to the Edinburgh convention, where he was arrested and convicted to 14 years transportation. He died within a year of arriving in Australia.

OTHER RADICAL FIGURES

Sir Francis Burdett (1770-1844) Educated at Westminster School and Oxford. He inherited, and married into, great fortune. Entered parliament in 1796 (buying his seat for £4000). Independent of both parties, he opposed the war with France and the suspension of Habeas Corpus, and denounced corruption. He became an effective and popular speaker in the democratic movement. He was defeated twice as candidate for Middlesex, but gained the Westminster seat in 1807 and kept it for 30 years. He became a leading exponent of moderate parliamentary reform though he played little part in the passing of the 1832 reform bill.

William Frend (1757-1841) Son of wine merchant (Canterbury). Studied mathematics at Cambridge. Ordained; appointed fellow of Jesus College in 1779. In 1787 he left the Church and joined the Unitarians. Campaigned against university rules precluding dissenters from taking degrees. His pamphlet *Peace & Union*, arguing for reforms of parliamentary representation, of the Law, and against religious discrimination, incensed the authorities and Frend was 'banished from the University'. He moved to London where he became involved in the anti-war and reform movements. He worked for the LCS though whether he actually joined is doubtful. He continued on the fringe of the reform movement for the rest of his life.

William Godwin (1756-1836) Came from a dissenting family in Norfolk and after studying at the Hoxton Academy, served for five years as Presbyterian minister. His reading of Rousseau, Helvetius et al., together with his close friendship with Thomas Holcroft, led to his turning atheist and republican. The French revolution sealed this conversion. In 1793 he produced *Enquiry concerning Political Justice* which, with his novel *The Adventures of Caleb Williams* (1794), enjoyed an enormous vogue, bringing him fame and riches (and later the title 'father of English anarchism'). But his following withered and he spent the rest of his life in relative obscurity. Despite his earlier condemnation of the institution of marriage, he married Mary Wollstonecraft in 1797, to legitimise their impending offspring. His wife died shortly after the birth of their daughter, Mary, who survived and later married the poet Shelley who was a great admirer of Godwin.

Richard Phillips (1767-1840) In 1788 moved to Leicester where he opened bookshop/lending library. 1792 established *Leicester Herald* with revolutionary sympathies. 1794 arrested & tried for selling Paine's *The Rights of Man*. Sentenced 18 months imprisonment. 1795 moved to London after his bookshop was destroyed by fire. 1805 established publishing business (authors included Godwin, Holcroft, Thelwall, Cartwright). 1807-8 served as sheriff. 1808 knighted. Another fire destroyed his printing premises. 1810 declared bankrupt. His political life over, he started literary journal *Monthly*. Turned to authorship and was moderately successful. Retired to Brighton where he died.

Richard Price (1723-91) Born in Llangeinor, Glamorgan. His father (Huw Prys) was a congregational minister. Price anglicised his name on moving to London where he was ordained as Presbyterian in 1744. He was full-time minister at Newington Green from 1758. His scholarly writings in science, theology, ethics and politics gave him a world-wide reputation – he was elected Fellow of the Royal Society in 1765 and was awarded a degree in Divinity at Aberdeen in 1769. He was awarded a LLD degree at Yale in 1781 and was made a member of the American Academy of Arts and Sciences in 1782. Enthusiastic supporter of the French revolution – his sermon, produced as a pamphlet, *Discourse on the Love of our Country*, provoked Burke to write *his Reflections on the Revolution in France*.

Joseph Priestley (1733-1804) Born nr Leeds, son of a weaver. Raised in dissenting atmosphere. Ordained in 1762. Elected to Royal Society on account of electrical experiments. Minister at Leeds 1767. Continued scientific work. Completed many publications on science and politics, the latter making him suspect to the government. Settled in Birmingham 1780. His political interventions included support of Wilkes and later the campaign to repeal of Test & Corporation Acts. Greeted French Revolution with enthusiastic favour, writing spirited reply to Burke. Suffered an attack by the Birmingham Church & King mobs in riots of 1791, his house and laboratory being burnt down. Made a French citizen in 1792 and was elected to the National Assembly. Emigrated to America in 1794 and spent his remaining years in Pennsylvania.

Christopher Wyvill (1740-1822) He came from a family of landed gentry. Educated at Queens College, Cambridge. Ordained 1763, but never a committed cleric. Married into money. He became leader of a movement of landowners, originating in Yorkshire, who wanted greater representation of the Counties, with annual parliaments to improve the economic management of the country. This movement became particularly active during the American war when landowners felt badly hit by taxes, and it attracted Whig support. Burke became its parliamentary spokesman. Wyvill continued to be active in the reform movement which culminated in the Reform Act of 1832.

Appendix 2

Notes about historical events relevant to this story

1685 James II succeeded to the throne on the death of his brother Charles II. His Catholicism brought him into conflict with the Protestant bishops. A plot was hatched to replace him: his son-in-law William, who had married his daughter Mary in 1677, and was at this time *statholder* of Holland, accepted an invitation to come and save England from 'Catholic tyranny'.

1688 William landed at Torbay on 5 November and headed for London. In the face of opposition by the Church and powerful peers, backed by popular rioting in London, James fled to France and William entered the capital on 9 December.

1689 The vacated throne was passed to William and his wife Mary jointly, on their signing a Declaration of Rights which asserted the 'true, antient and indubitable rights of the people of this realm', and declared, among other things, that no law should be enacted, or money levied, or standing army maintained, without the consent of Parliament. Elections of members of parliament were to be 'free', and there was to be free debate in parliament. It was made lawful to petition the sovereign. Juries were to be empanelled for every trial. This more or less completed what came to be known as the 'Glorious Revolution', which was subsequently celebrated as having happened in 1688.

1714 The throne passed to the House of Hanover when Queen Anne (Mary's sister) died without issue. The German-speaking George I took over, until his death in 1727 when he was succeeded by his son George II. It was an age of exploration and colonisation, notably in India and America. Boundary disputes with the French colonists in North America and the West Indies led in 1756 to the 'Seven Years War'.

1760 George III succeeded to the throne. The Duke of Newcastle was Prime Minister, though William Pitt (the Elder), Secretary of State (i.e. Foreign Secretary), was the real leader and was later credited with the glory that accrued from the ascendancy of British arms. He was rewarded in 1766 with a peerage, becoming Earl of Chatham. At this time parliament represented the interests of the landed gentry, members being elected by that minority of the male population who qualified for the vote by virtue of their property and/or income. There were two political groupings, the Whigs and the Tories, out of which the Liberal and Conservative parties grew in the nineteenth century. The Whigs had dominated since 1688 and George saw fit to redress this (to him) unwelcome imbalance by creating quite a large number of Tory peers.

1763-9 A member of Parliament, John Wilkes, caused a stir by publishing an article violently critical of the King, for which he was arrested and expelled from the Commons. He was however re-elected by the voters of Middlesex. He was expelled again and again re-elected. This was repeated a third time. It became a *cause célèbre*. The cry 'Wilkes for Freedom' expressed a growing frustration with the functioning of parliament.

1775-83 American War of Independence (see Chapter 10). The colonists revolted against the oppressive military rule left behind after the Seven Years War, and against heavy taxes imposed by the London government. The British attempted to suppress the revolt rather than negotiate a settlement, and this led to full-scale war. The colonists declared independence in 1776 and were supported by the French. The war was vehemently opposed by many in the home country (including Whig politicians). In 1782 the government of Lord North was defeated and replaced by a Whig administration under the Marquis of Rockingham, which included such eminent men as Charles Fox, Edmund Burke and Richard Sheridan. But Rockingham died only three months later and was succeeded by Lord Shelburne, who removed these luminaries. He appointed William Pitt (the Younger, 23 year-old son of the Earl of Chatham) as Chancellor of the Exchequer. Eventually, after a series of military defeats, the British were obliged to recognise the new independent state and thereafter their rule was confined to the northern territories (which became Canada) and to some of the islands of the West Indies.

1780 Yorkshire petition (organised by Wyvill) for parliamentary reform. Formation of Society for Constitutional Information (SCI), Gordon riots (see Chapter 11). London was terrorised by prolonged rioting instigated by Lord George Gordon's attacks on legislation to repeal penal laws against Roman Catholics. The disturbances were quelled, but remained a trauma in the communal memory.

1783 Pitt the Younger became Prime Minister.

1785 Pitt's second attempt at modest parliamentary reform defeated.

1788 First bout of 'insanity' of George III. A Regency was discussed, but the King recovered (1789) before this was necessary.

1789-95 French Revolution (Chapter 14). The storming of the Bastille in Paris (July 14) is generally taken to mark the beginning of the French Revolution, although there had been some earlier preliminaries. The country was near bankruptcy following the wars with the British and in May the French King (Louis XVI), hoping to enlist the resources of the aristocracy, resurrected the long-defunct 'Estates General' a Council of three 'Estates' (*Etats*) – the First Estate being the Nobles, the Second the Clergy and the Third the Commoners (in effect the middle-class lawyers and businessmen). After six weeks the latter, finding themselves expected to rubber-stamp the policies of the King and Church, broke away, declaring themselves a 'National Assembly'. They were joined by many clergy and some nobles, but more importantly their action focused popular unrest, turning the hunger riots into a revolution. The storming of the Bastille was a symbolic act that fired the nation, city workers and peasantry alike. This was not at all what the Third Estate had intended, but, in E. J. Hobsbawm's words: 'The peculiarity of the French Revolution is that one section of the liberal middle-class was prepared to remain revolutionary up to, and indeed beyond, the brink of anti-bourgeois revolution': these were the Jacobins, whose name came to stand for radical revolution everywhere. There was an attempt over the next two years to establish a constitutional monarchy, but this was frustrated partly by the King himself whose non-acquiescence was dramatically demonstrated by his attempt to flee the country in June 1791. His flight was however intercepted and he was brought back to Paris. At the same time there was a growing menace of invasion from France's neighbours whose aristocracies feared the spread of the revolutionary 'disease'. This threat, together with fears of a counter-revolution from within, encouraged the more militant to hold sway. The King was put on trial and in January 1793 was guillotined (his Queen, Marie Antoinette, suffered the same fate ten months later). So the 'Reign of Terror' was ushered in: the guillotine was now continuously busy. No-one could count themselves safe. First one faction, then another, was in ascendancy. For many months Robespierre was the seemingly impregnable leader of the Left but he had enemies, and even he was arrested, tried and guillotined. Eventually the moderates gained the upper hand and a new constitution was established in August 1795 which placed executive power in the hands of a 'Directory' of five. It was supported by the military, and it was now that Napoleon began to make his presence felt. He was in charge of the troops who quelled oppositional rioters in Paris with a 'whiff of grape-shot'.

1790 The French revolution had been greeted with delight by British reformers but with foreboding by others. The latter were headed by Burke whose book *Reflections on the Revolution in France* appeared in November 1790.

1791 A spate of pamphlets followed Burke's book. Most notable was Tom Paine's *The Rights of Man*, which was widely sold despite many prosecutions against booksellers who offered it. 'Church and King' riots in Birmingham and elsewhere attacked the radicals.

1792 Formation of London Corresponding Society (LCS) (Chapter 17).

1793 Execution of Louis XVI (see above), France declared war on Britain. Edinburgh convention assembled and was dispersed. Leaders were arrested and subsequently many were sentenced to transportation. The Government was now extremely nervous of revolutionary activity spreading to Britain.

1794 Leaders of LCS and SCI arrested and charged with high treason. Three of them (Hardy, Tooke & Thelwall) were tried but acquitted. The others were then discharged (Chapters 30ff).

1795 Widespread food riots and demonstrations against the war. Revival of the LCS. Mass meeting organised, which was followed by an attack on the King, giving government the excuse for introducing the repressive Two Acts.

1796-9 Napoleon's campaigns in Italy and Egypt. His successes put him in a powerful position politically, and on his return he was made First Consul of France, becoming a virtual dictator.

1797 Naval mutinies at Spithead and the Nore.

1798 Arrest of entire committee of LCS. Outbreak of Irish rebellion. Short-lived French invasion of Ireland.

1799 Irish rebellion crushed. Union of Great Britain and Ireland under the name of the 'United Kingdom'. LCS, United Irishmen, United Englishmen outlawed (Chapter 42).

1801 Pitt resigned. Peace with France concluded.

1803 War with France resumed.

1804 Pitt re-instated as Prime Minister. Renewed threat of invasion from France.

1805 Nelson's victory at Trafalgar virtually finished French sea-power. Renewed coalition of UK, Austria, Russia and Sweden, which was however dealt a crippling blow by Napoleon's victory at Austerlitz.

1806 Pitt died. Lord Grenville became Prime Minister with Fox as Foreign Secretary (the Ministry of All Talents). Fox died later in the year.

1807 Duke of Portland heads government.

1810 King suffered renewed attack of 'madness'.

APPENDIX 2

1811 Prince of Wales appointed Regent.

1812 Earl of Liverpool became premier. Luddite riots. Wellington's campaign in Spain. Napoleon advanced to Moscow and was then forced to retreat.

1814 Napoleon, after a series of reverses, abdicated. Banished to Elba.

1815 Napoleon escaped back to France and attempted to regain control. But he was defeated at Waterloo, and was banished to St Helena. Peace in Europe restored.

1815-20 Years of economic depression. Food riots. Renewed calls for parliamentary reform. Under Tory rule the fear of revolution was met by increased repressive measures. The 'Peterloo massacre' (1819) (see Chapter 43) was followed by the coercive 'Six Acts'.

1820 George III died. The Regent became George IV.

1821-31 Unrest abated with increasing prosperity, but there was a growing demand for parliamentary reform which led to the return of a Whig government pledged to reform.

1824 Cartwright died (Chapter 43).

1830 Accession of William IV.

1832 Reform Bill passed into law. Hardy died (Chapter 44).

Bibliography

PRIMARY SOURCES

Newspapers
Cambridge Chronicle, Examiner, Leicester Herald, Morning Post, Morning Chronicle, Northampton Mercury, Norwich Mercury, The Sun, The Times.

Books
Annual register 1794, London 1799.

John Binns, *Recollections of the Life of John Binns*, Philadelphia 1854.

Edmund Burke, *Reflections on the Revolution in France* [1790] Penguin edition 1969.

F. Cartwright, *The Life and Correspondence of John Cartwright* [1826] (2 vols) Reprinted New York 1969.

Thomas Cooper, *The Life of Thomas Cooper by Himself*, Hodder & Stoughton 1872.

R. Dinmore, A*n Exposition of the Principles of the English Jacobins*, Norwich 1796.

William Godwin, *Cursory Strictures ...*, reprinted in J. W. Marken & B. R. Pollin (eds),*Uncollected writings*, Gainesville 1968.

Thomas Hardy, *Memoir*, 1832. Reprinted D. Vincent 1977.

W. Haller & G. Davis (eds), *The Leveller Tracts 1647-1653*, reprinted Peter Smith, Gloucester, Mass. 1964.

George Herbert, *Shoemaker's Window*, Phillimore (for Banbury Historical Society) 1971.

T.B. & T.J. Howell, *State Trials*, vols 24, 25,London 1818.

Thomas Paine, *The Rights of Man* [1791] Penguin edition 1987.

—— *Common Sense* [1776] reprinted in *Political Writings*, CUP 1989.

Francis Place, *The Autobiography of Francis Place*, edited by Mary Thale, CUP 1972

Mary Thale (ed), *Selections from the Papers of the London Corresponding Society*, CUP 1983.

Mrs John Thelwall, *The life of John Thelwall*, 1837.

Secondary sources

G. E. Aylmer (ed), *The Levellers in the English Revolution* , Thames & Hudson 1975.

J. O. Baylen & N J. Grossman, *Biographical Dictionary of Modern British Radicals 1770-1830*, Harvester Press 1979.

P. A. Brown, *The French Revolution in English History*, London 1965.

C. B. Cone, *The English Jacobins*, New York, 1968.

Antonia Fraser, *The Gunpowder Plot*, Mandarin 1996.

Albert Goodwin, *Friends of Liberty*, Hutchinson 1979.

E. J. Hobsbawm, *The Age of Revolution 1789-1848* , Weidenfeld & Nicholson 1975.

Robert Hughes, *The Fatal Shore*, Collins Harvill 1987.

Frieda Knight, *University Rebel*, Gollancz 1971.

J. W. Osborne, *John Cartwright* , CUP 1972.

Temple Patterson, *Radical Leicester*, Leicester University Press 1954.

John Saville (ed), *Democracy and the Labour Movement* , Lawrence & Wishart 1954.

Simon Schama, *Citizens*, Viking 1989.

Howard Shaw, *The Levellers*, Longman 1968.

Olivia Smith, *The Politics of Language, 1791-1819*, OUP 1984.

E. P. Thompson, *The Making of the English Working Class*, Penguin 1988.

—— *The Romantics*, Merlin Press 1997.

Claire Tomalin, *The life and death of Mary Wollstonecraft*, Penguin, 1992

Alan Wharam, *The Treason Trials*, Leicester University Press 1992.

Gwyn Williams, *Artisans and Sans-Culottes* , Edward Arnold (Libris) 1989.

Index

---

* members of LCS
• members of SCI